What can ... with the kid who...?

BY THE SAME AUTHOR

Teaching the Unteachable

PRACTICAL IDEAS TO GIVE TEACHERS HOPE AND HELP WHEN
BEHAVIOUR MANAGEMENT STRATEGIES FAIL

Published by Worth Publishing 2009   ISBN 9781903269121

*"If only I'd had this book when I started my teaching career I would have
been more confident and happy as a teacher"*

Julie Blevins (Drama and English teacher, secondary school)

In the fast-paced, pressurised, often chaotic life of a school, there are times when even the best tried-and-tested ideas on behaviour management don't seem to work with some classes and some students. Even the most experienced teacher will have times when they feel de-skilled and incompetent.

Teacher and educational therapist, **Marie Delaney**, recognises the stresses and emotional demands affecting teachers today. In **TEACHING the UNTEACHABLE,** she provides a summary of effective behaviour management strategies, taken from individual 'real life' case studies and her own extensive experience. She then explores the reasons why they don't always work. Drawing on the most useful insights from therapy and psychology she offers an easily accessible framework for understanding the behaviour of those children and young people. Using practical examples, she shows how to use these ideas to reach 'unteachable' students. The author presents a way of thinking and a set of key skills to help teachers engage these pupils in learning. The result is a complete toolkit of skills that supports all teachers every day in the classroom

Contents include

- why some students are more difficult to teach ● what such children 'do' to us ● the effects of loss, separation, neglect and trauma on learning ● the way our emotions affect the management of relationships ● conscious and unconscious processes which affect readiness for teaching and learning ● developing skills and classroom strategies ● finding and using support
- ways for a teacher to reach and teach these children, whilst caring for ourselves and our colleagues

What can I do with the kid who…?

A teacher's quick guide to dealing
with disruptive pupils (and their parents)

MARIE DELANEY

www.worthpublishing.com

First published 2010 by Worth Publishing Ltd
www.worthpublishing.com

Printed in Great Britain by the MPG Books Group, Bodmin and Kings Lynn

British Library Cataloguing in Publication Data
A catalogue record for this book is available from the British Library

ISBN   9781903269145

Cover and text design by Anna Murphy

Dedicated to the memory of my father,

John Delaney

Acknowledgements

To the many children and young people with whom I have worked over the last twenty years. They have never ceased to amaze me, teach me and entertain me with their resilience, humour and perseverance. It is from them that I have learned the most. They are not mentioned here by name, but they are the main inspiration for this book.

To the colleagues who have helped me develop ideas and who have been prepared to try them out in difficult circumstances. In particular:

Colleagues at DYP. In particular, Paul Hill for supporting my early efforts with the 'unteachables', and Caitlin Walker, for her insight and inspiration in using Clean Language.

My many colleagues at Pilgrims Teacher Training, from whom I have learned so much about training and teaching. In particular to Simon Marshall for his insights into troubled families, Judy Baker for her help with NLP, Mario Rinvolucri for his support and promotion, and Paul Davis for his creative ideas and continuing encouragement.

The teachers from many different countries on the Pilgrims' 'Dealing with Difficult Learners' courses who have added their experience and knowledge to the ideas.

The staff and pupils at the Aveley School, in particular, to Julie Blevins for her friendship and commitment to 'giving it a go' and Patrick Halcrow who justified the belief in him.

The staff and pupils at Bower Park School, in particular Mary Morrison, Mary Higgins, Katie Conquest, Melanie Nash and Bev Mason for putting children first and for always being willing to try out even the most unconventional ideas.

The Learning Mentors and staff in the Havering Excellence Cluster, in particular,

Angie Brown for her unshakeable belief in the goodness of children, and her capacity for seeing the best in everyone.

Lecturers and fellow students at the Caspari Foundation, from whom I learned that therapy has something to offer education.

Colleagues involved in the Southend TAMHS project, in particular, Jenny Finch, for sharing her expertise and therapeutic insights, and Tess Boyes for her belief and commitment to the cause.

Staff and pupils at St Kevin's School, Cork who have been willing to try out ideas and new ways of thinking about very challenging behaviour. In particular, Brendan O'Brien, for his practical and emotional support, Nicola Patterson for her creativity and insight.

Staff and pupils of Ballincollig Youthreach who have always been prepared to try again with new strategies and approaches.

Jessica Nash for reminding me why we left the bank and what's important about being a teacher.

Friends and colleagues in Ireland who have taken risks on new ideas, in particular, Aileen Lyons and Sharon Lambert for their continuing support and great PR, Paul Murphy, and Emma Terry. For providing encouragement and cups of tea, Louise O'Keeffe, Catherine Collins, Mandy Collins and Breda Dooley.

My family, Mum, Dad, Jen and Aidan for their continuing love, belief in me and unwavering support.

Olly - for his love, encouragement and support, especially the dinners!

Andrea Perry for her superb editing and being able to make sense of the first draft.

Martin Wood at Worth Publishing for first recognising the potential writer in me and his complete commitment to our projects.

Biography

Marie Delaney is an Educational Psychotherapist, teacher and teacher trainer. She has extensive experience of working with challenging behaviour - both pupils and staff! She is currently Director of the Learning Harbour, Crosshaven, Cork, Ireland and is working in a range of settings, both in Ireland and the UK. These include secure units, alternative education placements, youth justice projects, mainstream primary and secondary education as well as private practice. She has trained teachers in several countries and now offers consultancy, training and workshops across the education, social service and youth justice sectors. She is particularly interested in bringing therapeutic thinking into mainstream education in order to help teachers deal with challenging behaviour in the classroom. She is the author of *Teaching the Unteachable*, 2009, Worth Publishing.

AUTHOR NOTES

1 To protect the confidentiality of individual children, young people, carers or professionals, names and autobiographical details have been altered in every case quoted. Any case examples written are composite and drawn from a number of similar examples known to the author from her experience over many years of working with children and adolescents.

2 To simplify the text, the male gender is used on occasion to represent the child or young person, and the female gender to represent educational staff. No prejudice is implied by this.

3 To simplify the text, the term 'parent' is used on occasion to represent those now providing the primary care for children or young people. This term will therefore include adoptive parents, foster carers, family and friends

Contents

(continues ...)

What can I do with the kid who …

Activities and games

What can I do with the kid who…?

Chapter 1

Introduction "What can I do with the kid who…?"

This is a book for all those teachers and staff in schools who have ever uttered the weary cry, *"What can I do with the kid who …?"*. In my experience as a teacher and teacher trainer, this is the question asked most often by exasperated teachers around the world.

There are only seven kids in this book, each presenting a different kind of behaviour. I've deliberately chosen to address this small number, as they seem to reflect the behaviors that the majority of staff find universally challenging and difficult to deal with - bullying, resisting instruction, rubbishing work, continually calling out, and so on.

The strategies suggested in this book are not designed to replace other behaviour management techniques. Teachers usually know the basics of good behaviour management, and, on good days, can use them successfully with most children. But there are always some children whose behaviour doesn't seem to respond to normal class rules, and whom we continually seem to be correcting, cajoling, getting frustrated with, worried about, or even frightened by, the ones we're always discussing in our staffrooms. We also spend immense amounts of time on 'phone calls and in meetings with the parents and carers of these pupils. These are the children, adolescents and families in the chapters of this book.

In my previous book, *Teaching the Unteachable* (2009), I presented ideas from therapeutic training which I had learnt could help with challenging classroom behaviour. Some of this thinking is applied in the examples which follow. However, *What Can I Do With The Kid Who …?* has arisen in response to the questions asked by teachers in my workshops who have read *Teaching the Unteachable*, agreed with the ideas, but who wanted a clear follow-on set of practical suggestions based on what can be observed in class, without necessarily knowing much about a pupil's background. After all, in a busy school day, we can't always know or remember the history of all our pupils, particularly those whose troubled lives may be constantly changing.

Why should you take the time to read this book?

We spend a lot of time dealing with a relatively small number of these kids. It's often exhausting and de-motivating, affecting a disproportionate amount of our feeling about teaching. These pupils remain in our minds long after our classes with them have finished. We metaphorically 'take them home' with us: sometimes we may even find it hard to remember the positive parts of our day, because the interactions with our more challenging pupils have taken over our minds.

If we can take the time to try new ways of thinking about these kids, it might lead us to develop different and more creative strategies, save us time, and be less emotionally draining. This should impact positively on our emotional and physical readiness for teaching, and on the other learners in the class. Then we might be able to leave work behind and enjoy our home life, without those constant niggling doubts about our abilities to cope with some of the kids at school.

The ideas presented in this book are based on developing skills of *noticing* behaviour in a different way: *thinking about* our response to it: *taking account of* the feelings which seem to be triggered by it: and, only then, creating a bank of teaching strategies to deal with it. I will be using a format which I have called the **RETHINK** model, designed to provide you with a simple, structured approach to addressing behaviour. The four elements in this model are **Review, Reframe, Reflect** and **Respond.** There are **ten principles** which underpin the **RETHINK** model and it's important to bear these in mind when reading the chapters in this book. The model also draws on **four frameworks** for understanding what drives behaviour (*pp. 19-32*).

The ten principles

PRINCIPLE 1 Behaviour can be a form of communication about a child's needs unmet in their early years

PRINCIPLE 2 Children without boundaries will go in search of them

PRINCIPLE 3 There are two people in the teaching/learning relationship

PRINCIPLE 4 It is essential to stay in the learning zone

PRINCIPLE 5 We cannot change children and young people, only our reaction to them: but what we do may well create the possibility of them doing things differently

PRINCIPLE 6 Curiosity is core to working with challenging behaviour

PRINCIPLE 7 Non-judgmental descriptions can help us find effective solutions

PRINCIPLE 8 A trial-and-error approach is most productive

PRINCIPLE 9 Holding onto the ability to think, and not just react, is crucial

PRINCIPLE 10 We need to notice what is working and do more of it

The four theoretical frameworks

Where the feelings come from
The effects of trauma on learning
Attachment Patterns
The stages of play development

Taken together, all these components can give us the information we need to develop a new set of teaching strategies. Because teachers often say, *"I can understand the need to think differently, but in the heat of the moment, it's really difficult to think 'on-the-spot' and come up with the right thing to say"*, this book will suggest some instant verbal responses, as well as strategies which can be incorporated into lesson planning.

By taking the time to read this book, it's my hope and belief that you'll be able to spend less time feeling frustrated and de-skilled by the challenging behaviour of some of your pupils, and more time on creating an enjoyable, productive learning environment for all.

THE PRINCIPLES EXPLORED

PRINCIPLE I
Behaviour can be a form of communication about
a child's needs unmet in their early years

Challenging behaviour can tell us something about the pupil's unmet needs. This doesn't mean pupils are *deliberately* behaving in a certain way, but if we choose to interpret the behaviour as an attempt to *communicate a need* to us, or to seek fulfillment of the need, we may be able to increase our understanding of what's happening for the child in the learning situation. We may not know much about our pupil's early childhood experience, but their behaviour may be telling us something important about it.

Many of our pupils haven't had the opportunity to acquire the necessary skills to become successful learners (*see p.23*). They've often missed out on key experiences in their early years which would have enabled them to develop the social and emotional competence essential to being able to learn in a classroom setting.

Other pupils have been affected by difficult, traumatic and insecure attachment experiences when very young (*see p.23, 27*), and have learned not to trust relationships with adults. This will affect their classroom learning, as teachers very often represent key attachment figures.

Thus both groups of pupils will unconsciously strive to find other ways to fulfill their unique unmet needs in our schools: needs such as the experience of learning how to learn, or for secure attachment. We can help them to have a different experience of the relationship with both the teacher and the task in our work in our classrooms.

So the three key questions we'll be addressing about a child's behaviour in every chapter in this book are as follows:

> **What is the UNMET NEED the child is trying to fulfill through this behaviour?**
>
> **What has this child NOT had experience of?**
>
> **What is it that this child CANNOT believe about the teacher and the classroom?**

PRINCIPLE 2
Children without boundaries
will go in search of them

We need to ensure our classroom management is clear and consistent, and that boundaries are explicit. I am assuming that as a teacher reading this, you'll already have a range of good behaviour management strategies with which to control your classes. For example, you'll have:

→ clear routines established for different stages of the lesson: getting silence, stopping activities, beginning and ending lessons, coming in and out of the room

→   a few clear rules with consistent sanctions and rewards

→   knowledge of how to give clear instructions, demonstrated and checked by giving and getting examples, or getting students to repeat the instructions back to you

→   skills for planning organised lessons, catering to different learning styles

→   clear department plans and routines for removal of disruptive pupils from lessons where necessary

PRINCIPLE 3
There are two people in the teaching/learning relationship

Challenging behaviour is very emotive, and we will have a range of feelings around it. Sometimes these feelings belong to us - when we're tired, frustrated, worried (about what's happening, and/or possibly about something other than the present situation) - and sometimes they may be coming from the pupils (*see p.22*). We need to look at our own behaviour, feelings and responses as well as those of the pupils. We need to be able to understand and manage our own internal emotions and external reactions in order to deal with those of our pupils (*for more ideas on managing your own internal and external states, see Appendix B*).

PRINCIPLE 4
It is essential to stay in the learning zone

Don't let the learning zone become a battle zone. The primary task of schools is to facilitate learning. Our primary task is teaching, and the pupils' primary task is learning. *With certain pupils it is all too easy for the focus to shift from learning to conflict.* We need to find strategies which don't allow a problematic learning situation to escalate into conflict.

PRINCIPLE 5

We cannot change children and young people,
only our reaction to them:
but what we do may well create the possibility
of them doing things differently

We need to focus on what is within our control. We need to set ourselves goals where
we know how to take the first step, *and* it is a step which is within our control. Often
we set goals which involve waiting for someone else to take the first step or which
require that person to change first. For example, you might decide that your goal for
a pupil is that *"He needs to learn to listen"*. This is only within the control of the
pupil and not you, the teacher. If you think about what you really want, you might
set the goal as *"I will ask him to show me he is listening in class in a way which I
understand"*. The first step of this is within your control.

 We need to be aware of our own triggers*. Some types of challenging behaviour
will spark certain responses in us. These triggers are different for everyone. The more
aware we become of our own triggers, the better we will be able to manage them and
respond appropriately in challenging situations.

PRINCIPLE 6

Curiosity is core to working
with challenging behaviour

We can't have all the answers or know what is going on in the minds of our students.
We can, however, be curious, and collect information to help us understand what's
happening. Keeping a sense of curiosity and interest in a pattern of behaviour will

---

** By 'our own triggers', I mean a type of behaviour which always seems to get under our skin; it quickly sparks
an unconscious learned response in us, which isn't helpful in managing the behaviour and makes it difficult for
us to think clearly and impartially about what's happening. For example, I know that I find it difficult to deal
with pupils who always seem to feel sorry for themselves, saying that everyone hates them and there's nothing
good about school. I worked with a colleague who was very sympathetic to these pupils, and was much better at
dealing with their problems than I was.*

help us deal with it differently. Not knowing the answer can feel very frustrating for us as teachers. When dealing with challenging behaviour, we need to allow ourselves a state of *'wondering about'* and *'not knowing'*. Whatever we observe is useful information.

PRINCIPLE 7
Non-judgmental descriptions can help
us find effective solutions

We need to be able to describe our pupils' challenging behaviour without jumping to an instant interpretation or judgment of it. When we find ourselves in conflict or in problematic situations, our normal human reaction is to judge the other person and their behaviour. However, blaming is unhelpful, and doesn't lead us to solutions. We can end up being quite rigid in our opinions about each other, stuck in our thinking about 'the other side', and unable to see what is actually happening.

PRINCIPLE 8
A trial-and-error approach
is most productive

There is no magical solution to difficult behaviour. As teaching/educational staff, we are dealing with people and relationships, not machines and formulae. It's not as easy as ABC - in an ideal world, do A, and then B will always happen, and then C: but we know it's not like that. Classroom teaching is about establishing, maintaining and repairing relationships. It is important to reflect on what happens, and see 'failure' as feedback to put back into our thinking framework. Relapse is an important part of learning. We often learn the most when things go wrong. Maybe 'failure' is a sign that we don't need to try harder, but rather, start approaching the situation from a slightly different perspective, in a slightly different direction.

PRINCIPLE 9
Holding onto the ability to think, and
not just react, is crucial

When we feel challenged by a pupil's behaviour, and under pressure because of it, our thinking can be 'hijacked' by upset, angry emotions and feelings. This can lead to reflexive action driven by the desire to sort things out immediately. We need to be able to just pause for a moment - if only for a second - and find ways to hold onto our 'thinking adult', by which I mean staying connected to that part of ourselves which can separate out our own emotions from the realities of the situation, and think more objectively about the child's needs.

In order for this to happen, we need to decide that it is OK to allow time for thinking, and then plan this time into our work. A normal school day is hectic and can be quite fraught. We rarely make time to stop and think . Yet we know we need to find this time to create thinking spaces around the pupils and their presenting behaviour, which is 'taking over' our own minds; otherwise we'll see the problem, and want to jump quickly to finding a solution.

With our most challenging pupils, we need to take that step back: explore the issue, think differently, try to understand it from different perspectives: and then, maybe only then, generate some strategies. This book provides a 'thinking framework' which can be applied to each situation.

Many of the responses suggested in the following chapters assume that the teacher is *thinking aloud with the pupil* about their behaviour. We need to find ways to involve the pupil in the thinking, and create meaningful dialogues between us. We don't need to be all-knowing. We do need to be open to new thinking. Many of these children haven't had the experience of a thinking adult staying alongside them and being willing to try to make sense of their random and often anxious thoughts.

PRINCIPLE 10
We need to notice
what is working

We tend to dwell on what's going wrong, and the times when the pupil isn't behaving appropriately. By finding a way to notice what *is* working, we may find new strategies and new insights. We also need to notice progress, however small. When a pupil is misbehaving, we notice it. When the same child is *not* misbehaving, we often don't notice it. There will be times when the child is NOT 'doing' the challenging behaviour: this needs to be noticed as evidence to inform our framework of thinking, as much as it is to let the child know we see all sides of them. So each chapter will end with some signs of progress for '*The kid who ...*', signs that can give you confidence that the changes *you've* made in how *you* work really are helping.

A fluid process

It's important to recognise that it won't be necessary to go through every stage of the process for every pupil. For some pupils, you'll only need to use Stage 1, **reviewing** the present situation, to develop new responses which have a positive effect in stopping or minimising the pupil's inappropriate behaviour. However, that may not be enough. Some pupils don't respond to the strategies in Stage 1, most of which are connected to **reviewing** classroom management strategies and behavioural responses. With these pupils, it will be necessary to continue through the process, asking different questions at Stage 2, and developing a different set of responses. These may help; but remember, it's not a linear process, so trial and error will be needed, because each child is different. So there will still be some pupils with whom you'll need to go all the way to Stage 3, to **reflect** on the potential underlying causes of their behaviour. Reflection at Stage 3 will also give you new options, new ways of viewing what's happening, and new ways to **respond**, all of which will help you learn more about the child and their learning needs at every level.

The **RETHINK** model

The **RETHINK** model can be seen as a fluid process, not a linear progression. Each of the first three stages of the process involves looking at the pupil and their behaviour in a certain way, and developing responses based on the results of our new perspective at each stage.

REVIEW

Review what is already happening in the classroom with this pupil, particularly in relation to classroom management and current teacher/whole school responses to their behaviour

REFRAME

Reframe the behaviour and your own thinking, in order to find new insights and ways forward

REFLECT

Take some time to reflect on what might be underlying the behaviour: in particular, the child's unmet needs and the feelings involved in your interaction with them

RESPOND

After each of the three preceding stages, develop responses which are appropriate to that stage. These will be both responses made verbally, and responses which will involve changes in your lesson planning

THE STAGES of the RETHINK model explained

STAGE I *REVIEW*

Review what is happening in the class at the moment

CLASSROOM MANAGEMENT

The first stage of our thinking must be to **review** what's happening with this pupil in class and around the school at the moment. This might seem obvious, but it often gets lost in the maelstrom of emotions that challenging behaviour can evoke in us.

Firstly, it is vitally important that we hold onto our consistent classroom management with these pupils, and that they understand this. So the initial step must be to **review** the consistency of our own classroom management: if necessary, restate the classroom rules, making sure rewards and sanctions are being applied: ensuring all the time that the school behaviour policy is being used effectively. At this stage, we also need to ensure that all our pupils are aware of these rules and their consequences.

It will also be important to **review** any plans which are already in place with regard to a particular pupil, who else is involved, and how such plans are being monitored. This should involve checking if the problem with the child is universal, in most classes, or particular to a certain lesson, subject, time of day or member of staff.

We should also **review** what response the current behaviour gets in our class. A child who is misbehaving might be getting a lot of attention from a teacher, and then does *not* get attention when they are behaving appropriately. He or she is unlikely to have any motivation to change their inappropriate behaviour if it is getting them what they need.

Having taken the time to **review** these aspects, we may find that becoming clearer and more consistent in our response to behaviour will be effective in managing it better. However, if the pupil doesn't respond to our usual classroom management techniques, we'll need to go on to the next step in the process.

STAGE 2 *REFRAME*

When we're having problems dealing with a certain type of behaviour, we tend to get rather stuck in our thinking. We try all the strategies we know, and we ask colleagues for their suggestions. Sometimes this can help. However, we often end up simply doing more of the same thing, the thing which isn't working.

In the **RETHINK** model, the next step, **reframing,** involves choosing to think completely differently about the pupils, the behaviour and our interaction with them. Some pupils seem to be quite literally 'on another planet' to the rest of us, so we may need to expand our own thinking in ways which seem alien to us in order to come up with **reframes**.

The essential method of **reframing** used in this book is to:

→   *describe the behaviour* specifically and objectively, separating these
     descriptions out from interpretations of the behaviour and judgments about it
→   *find a positive intention in the behaviour*, and react accordingly.
     On occasion, this will involve a huge stretch of the imagination, but it
     can often bring the best results. How we interpret a behaviour will affect
     our response to it. For example, if I choose to believe that a pupil is
     deliberately trying to provoke me, I will probably react in a fairly negative
     and punitive way. If I choose to believe the same pupil is trying to engage
     in their relationship with me because it's important to them, however,
     I will react more positively to essentially the same behaviour. As I can
     never know for certain what the pupil's intention is, choosing the more
     positive interpretation should help me develop a more positive response
→   *name the feelings you are having,* and take some time to think about
     where these are coming from. Even if they are very negative feelings,
     they're important. Often we try to overcome or 'get over' these kinds
     of feelings, but in this model, they're seen as important information for

understanding what is happening in the classroom. If we can name the feelings for ourselves, we can then develop responses which will help the pupils understand what is happening to them. We might decide to name the feelings for the pupil, or we might simply decide to use the information for ourselves. It can be a relief, for example, to realise that if you are feeling like a failure, this could well be a reflection of what the pupil is feeling themselves.

When you've **reframed** what's happening in the classroom, you can now develop responses and strategies based on this new perspective. You may find this will lead to successful interventions with the pupil. However, once again, you may find that a pupil doesn't respond to the strategies you've developed in **reframing**. You may need to go on to the third stage of the process, **reflection** on the child's unmet needs.

STAGE 3 *REFLECT*

The **reflection** part of this approach focuses on the child's needs and possible early experiences. I won't be suggesting that you need to know everything about the child's life to date, but that you take some time to **reflect** on what their behaviour might be showing you in relation to the skills, the beliefs about relationships with adults and the expectations they have of those relationships, which the child has and has not acquired in their early years. When **reflecting** on the child's needs, I will use the four frameworks listed on p.3 (*and described in detail on pp.19-33*) to give some structure to the process and new insight into what is driving the child's behaviour, often unconsciously.

Essentially, some children will have had traumatic early experiences which may have taught them that it isn't safe to trust relationships, that adults aren't there to nurture and protect. They may have had little or no experience of an adult trying to understand them and their feelings, or trying to give a name to these feelings.

We learn to think by being thought about, and these children may well not have had this experience. This could have been for a variety of reasons, but the risk factors I will describe in this book are domestic violence, loss, trauma, addiction, and parental mental illness (*for more detailed explanation see p.23*)

Children with these elements in their background will find it hard to behave appropriately in class, as they've learned it's not safe to take risks, to wait for attention, to make mistakes, to ask for help - all key skills involved in making use of the classroom environment and relationship.

STAGE 4 *RESPOND*

The fourth **R** in the **RETHINK** model is **respond**, applicable after any or all of the preceding three stages. As I explained on p.10, it won't always be necessary to go through the whole process of **reviewing**, **reframing** and **reflecting** on the needs with every challenging pupil, because at each stage you'll be developing a specific bank of strategies to **respond** to your new perspective on the child, and implementing these strategies may be effective at an earlier stage.

In each of the following 7 chapters, I will use the **RETHINK** approach to illustrate how this way of thinking can help us develop a range of teaching strategies for dealing with specific types of challenging behaviour. Chapter 9 will also suggest positive strategies for dealing with challenges from parents/carers, and Chapter 10 will offer further strategies to help us develop effective working relationships with colleagues who may be suspicious of these new ways of thinking. Both these situations can present us with problems at times. After each of the three stages, **review**, **reframe** and **reflect,** possible **responses** will be suggested in a bank of teaching strategies.

It isn't necessary to read every chapter straight through to acquire an understanding of how to apply this model. Initially, you'll probably find it helpful to focus on the chapters which relate to the classroom behaviour you are finding difficult, and learn about the model through applying the strategies. But although the cases are all different, each chapter follows the format summarised above - The **RETHINK** model:

REVIEW	what you are doing at the moment
REFRAME	the behaviour and your thinking about it
REFLECT	on the your own feelings and the pupil's needs
RESPOND	to the pupil's behaviour in a different way

It is my hope that this will become an automatic approach for you in thinking about challenging behaviour in your classroom.

Strategies

Each chapter will suggest a bank of strategies related to the different sections of the framework. Some will seem more relevant to you than others. They are not meant to be an exhaustive list, but an indication of ideas you might try. You'll probably feel more comfortable with some than others, but it may be important to try something that seems strange initially, as this might be an effective solution. Sometimes we encounter difficulties because what is happening or how to respond to it is quite literally beyond our imagination, outside the frame of thinking we usually use to come up with a strategy. Don't dismiss an idea just because it doesn't seem familiar, you don't like the sound of it, or are not sure how it would work. Experiment. Try it out. Notice what happens. Use the feedback to develop your own responses.

Checklist

In Appendix A, you'll find a checklist for you to use if you wish when thinking about any child with challenging behaviour in your classroom. The checklist is designed as an aide-memoire to guide you through the application of the **RETHINK** model.

You may find it useful to use this checklist when you're feeling 'stuck' in your work with a child and want a structured thinking approach.

And finally ...

There are no easy solutions to challenging behaviour, because we're often dealing with children with very complex needs and backgrounds. It might sometimes seem that those of us who work in schools are being asked to fix the woes of the world, to have a 'magic dust' to sprinkle on children who find school difficult. However, we need to realise that for many children, school is still the most important and safest place to be. Staff in schools have huge influence over a child's social and emotional development, as well as their academic needs. We all know a teacher who changed our lives. It really is possible for teachers to help a child understand and change their behaviour, so that the child's life chances are improved, and he or she can begin to have hope for a better future.

I hope, by reading this book, you'll be inspired to keep on doing this!

THE FOUR FRAMEWORKS

FRAMEWORK 1

WHERE THE FEELINGS COME FROM

Noticing feelings and patterns of interaction

When we're dealing with challenging behaviour, we can often have very strong, almost unbearable feelings ourselves. We may feel frustrated, helpless, inadequate and incompetent. The children will also have overwhelming feelings, as will their parents, and very often our colleagues and staff from other agencies working with the family will too. It can feel as if everyone is failing and falling apart, which can lead to angry, frustrating interactions in class, and equally frustrating meetings with parents, colleagues or other agencies.

Strong feelings often get in the way of thinking rationally. They can sometimes provoke us into reactive, knee-jerk approaches rather than more pro-active, thoughtful ones. If we take time to notice and understand our feelings, we are likely to be freed up to think more productively about the situation. We need to be aware of what might be stirring these powerful feelings, because they may be giving us valuable information about what's happening in the child's internal world.

In the first instance, we need to accept that strong feelings may come from us, particularly if we're having a stressful day. So we need to be aware of and acknowledge our own personal 'buttons': certain children and certain behaviours will trigger reactions in us more than others, especially at times when we have a lot going on in our own personal or professional lives.

However, when faced with dealing with challenging behaviour in the classroom, the feelings we experience may not originate from us. They may be an example of what Freud called 'unconscious defence mechanisms' (1973). When any of us feel overwhelmed by an emotion, we may sometimes need to do something to defend against having the experience. Unconsciously, if we can't cope with the feeling and need to off-load it somehow, we try to get rid of it. In the case studies which follow, you'll see that these mechanisms appear in our classrooms, when children feel overwhelmed by what they are struggling with. What you experience may well be related to the child's experience, and is information for you about what is happening for them rather than something to try to suppress or overlook.

In each chapter, I'll show how to deal with these feelings and, where appropriate, how to acknowledge them in your teaching.

Unconscious processes and defence mechanisms

- Transference and counter-transference
  (Ch. 2, p.42-3, Ch. 5, p.90-2, Ch. 7, p.118, Ch. 9, p.146, 157)
- Projection (Ch 3, p.56-7, 61-2, Ch. 4, p.70-1, Ch. 5, p.90, Ch.7, p.120, 126, Ch. 9, p.143, 146-7, Ch. 10, p.170-1, 178)
- Displacement (Ch. 3, p.58, 61, Ch.9, p.149, 157, 163, Ch. 10, p.170-1, 175)
- Omnipotence (Ch. 8, p.133)
- Splitting (Ch. 9, p.155, 163, Ch.10, p.178)

FRAMEWORK 2

THE EFFECTS OF SPECIFIC TYPES OF TRAUMA ON CLASSROOM LEARNING

Why some children find it hard to learn in a classroom

For whatever reason, the children in this book and others like them haven't learned the skills they need to be successful in a classroom. Their behaviour shows us that there are gaps in their social and emotional skills, which are affecting their ability to settle into learning. In order to understand what these gaps might be, we need to take a step back for a moment, and think about how children normally become good learners. They will usually have had early childhood experiences which allow them to:

- feel safe in learning new skills and be willing to take risks
- have good self-esteem
- be able to seek help when needed, without expecting criticism or ridicule
- be able to concentrate and ignore distractions
- be able to manage frustration, anxiety and disappointment
- have the capacity to bear not knowing
- be optimistic and have a positive attitude to a problem
- be capable of waiting for attention

But there will be children in our classes who haven't had the kind of experience in their early childhood through which they could learn these skills. In fact, their life experience may have taught them quite the opposite: that relationships can't be trusted, that taking risks will lead to failure and humiliation, that asking for help leads to ridicule or being ignored, and that if you wait, you'll get overlooked.

Moreover, children whose minds are full up with other thoughts and worries about their life outside school can find it extremely difficult to focus in our classrooms. Their minds may be preoccupied with the struggle of living with domestic violence, loss, neglect, addiction, mental illness or abuse. They will have developed learned responses which served them more or less adequately in these difficult situations, but which simply don't work in school. Let's look briefly at how specific types of trauma and loss can affect classroom behaviour and learning.

Children affected by domestic violence

Children who have witnessed or been subjected to domestic violence will have experienced a huge range of conflicting emotions and feelings. They may have feelings of anger towards both parents: towards the victim for somehow 'allowing' the violence, and towards the aggressor for causing the abuse. This can cause a huge level of anxiety and confusion in their brains. These feelings cannot safely be expressed at home and they often come out in school. Children and adolescents living with this kind of experience may unconsciously re-create violent interactions with adults in school, since, on some level, this is what their brains have become accustomed to. They may appear aggressive or persecutory in school, seeming to empathise with the aggressor, and may despise what they see as weakness in others, causing them to bully other weaker or 'different' children (or the teacher). They will not necessarily respond to well-meaning adults in school. Why should they trust praise and gentleness? This is not what their lives have conditioned them to understand. (See Peter, Chapter 5, Brian, Chapter 7)

Children affected by loss

Many children in our classrooms have experienced loss and rejection of some kind: some may have had multiple instances through their short lives. Loss might be through bereavement, but could also include changes brought on by divorce, separation, fostering and adoption, having a family member in prison, family upheaval and/or the continual moving of the family home. These children may become very controlling, not wanting to admit that they need anyone to help them learn. This can express itself in the classroom as seeming indifference towards those trying to help them. They can seem very rejecting of the teacher. Indeed, why should they accept and trust this relationship, when they have lost people from previous close relationships?

Many of these children find change very hard to cope with, as they associate it with people going away and sudden, unexplained loss. They react badly to changes of routine and teaching. As they have come to expect catastrophe to strike at any moment, they may not be willing to take risks to learn, refusing to move on to new things. They may sometimes react angrily to offers of help, because they have aggressive feelings churned up inside them relating to unexpressed feelings of rage at a parent or loved one for leaving them. Of course there may also be huge sadness at the loss. These conflicting feelings can be particularly confusing if the parent has taken their own life or died through an addiction, been convicted of a crime or been abusive. These mixed up, chaotic feelings will make it difficult to settle in class and trust relationships with the staff. Children and adolescents with this kind of background may appear focused on the task, but only as long as it does not require asking for and accepting help. *(See Jamie, Chapter 3, Nikki, Chapter 8)*

Children affected by addiction

Children who have lived with a parent who is suffering from an addiction, such as drugs or alcohol, may not have experienced a consistent response from that adult in their early years. They will have experienced times when the adult was available to them and able to respond to their needs, particularly if the parent has been through periods of detox and trying to get clean from addiction. However, there will have been other times when the parent was unavailable emotionally and perhaps physically, so that the child's needs were not being met.

In class, these children may not appear to respond to consistent care and rules. They do not necessarily trust them. They expect every day to be different, and will sometimes unconsciously provoke staff into inconsistencies. They may have highs and lows in their own moods. They will seem hard to teach, as we can't predict their response from one day to the next. For them, inconsistency is the norm. (*See Lee, Chapter 2, Megan, Chapter 5*)

Children affected by parental mental illness

There will be some children in our classes who do not 'act out'. They may appear quiet and withdrawn, or indeed, like the 'perfect' student. Children who have dealt or are dealing with a parental mental illness can exhibit this kind of behaviour. They may have learned that their needs will be too overwhelming and worrying for their parent, so they want to make sure they are not a burden. This can present in class as a withdrawal from the relationship with the teacher. In addition, it might appear as a desire to keep everything very neat, tidy and under control.

They may also be excessively anxious but will not necessarily appear so. This means that in class, they may appear very calm and then suddenly have eruptions of anger or crying over quite a small incident. In their world, they find it hard to distinguish between an ordinary sad feeling and a complete disaster, so they damp down those feelings until they 'leak' out. They may be liable to self-harm. As with the group described above, children affected by parental mental illness may not have experienced an adult who can 'contain' their feelings, and will find it hard to admit to any problems when asked by an adult. By 'contain', I mean recognising the child's feelings, trying to understand and name them; and, if appropriate, reflecting them back to the child in a safe and manageable way (that is, talk about what's happening with the child in a relaxed, non-judgmental tone of voice: "*I can see you're angry at the moment. I'm wondering if you're also feeling a bit let down*"). (*See John, Chapter 4*)

FRAMEWORK 3

ATTACHMENT PATTERNS

Attachment Theory and the Learning Triangle

In some of my suggestions for thinking about these children and their challenging behaviour, I am using the model of the *Learning Triangle* as described by Geddes (2006). This triangle is based on the core concepts of Attachment Theory (Bowlby 1988), and ideas about how early attachment experiences affect a child's ability to learn in school. I will give a short overview here of the main points, but for more detailed information, please see Geddes, 2006 and Bombèr, 2007.

The Learning Triangle

In any learning experience, according to Geddes (2006), there is a triangle formed between teacher, pupil and task (*see below*). In order to learn, the pupil needs to feel secure and trust the relationship with the teacher. However, he or she also needs to be able to *separate* from the teacher and work on the task on his or her own, secure in the knowledge that the teacher is available to provide help and support when required. Children who have had secure experiences in their early lives are able to do both these things, and consequently can make the most of the school environment academically and socially. However, children who have not experienced this type of relationship with an adult in their early life can find it very difficult to make space inside themselves for the task of learning.

For example, some pupils may be over-anxious about maintaining and checking out the relationship with the teacher, continually seeking her reassurance and attention. They are unable to focus on any learning task which might distract them from this focus. This will show up in class as incessant calling out, an inability to start the task, turning up outside the staffroom at lunchtime looking for the teacher, and then becoming excessively upset if not given constant attention. They will rarely get a task finished, as they're constantly checking back with the teacher.

These pupils may not have had any experience of a primary caregiver consistently thinking about them and attending to their needs, what Bion (1962) calls 'holding them in mind'. This may be as a result of parental addiction or mental health issues, as we saw in Framework 2. Essentially, they can't believe that the teacher will remember them when not in their immediate vicinity. Such behaviour can be categorised as exhibiting a pattern of *insecure/ambivalent-resistant* attachment. (*See Lee, Chapter 2, Megan, Chapter 6*)

Other pupils may be unable to trust the relationship with their teacher: they have learned in their early years that they might be rejected in their attempts to seek attachment. Their early needs for care and attention have not been met. They may even have been rebuffed. This may be a result of living with domestic violence or as above, parental depression, (*see Framework* 2). They will reject the teacher-learner relationship. They will focus on a task, but this will only be possible for them as long as they don't need to ask for help. They'll often insist on doing the same task over and over again. They will sometimes start writing in their books before the task has been set, simply doing a task from the previous lesson. They will insist they don't need help, and often reject the presence of a teaching assistant assigned to help them. This can be categorised as an *insecure/avoidant pattern* of attachment. (*See Jamie, Chapter 3, John, Chapter 4, Nikki, Chapter 8*)

A third group of pupils may be displaying an *insecure/disorganised* pattern of behaviour. What these pupils do can be very unpredictable. They have problems with both the task *and* the relationship. Sometimes they are compliant and work well, other days they seem totally out of control and exhibit worrying behaviours such as banging their heads against the wall in frustration. These pupils have usually experienced very traumatising, abusive

environments and need to know that school itself is a safe and containing structure.
(*See Peter, Chapter 5, Brian, Chapter 7*)

The Learning Triangle

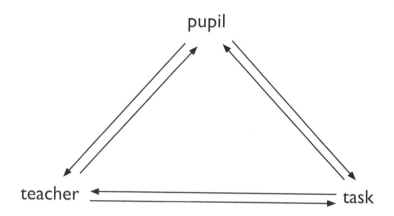

(Geddes, 2006 p.4)

If we look at a pupil's challenging behaviour from an attachment perspective, reflecting on how he or she deals with relationships and tasks in school, we may get some insight into their underlying attachment needs. Fundamentally, these needs are to have stable, reliable, consistent relationships with an empathic adult, which will free them both to settle to learn and to be at ease in the social environment of school. We can then build our strategies around this. We can ask the questions -

- Is the pupil trying to seek the relationship, or avoid it?
- Can he or she make use of the relationship with the teacher, or can he or she make use of the task to learn?
- Is this pattern consistent?

(for a more in-depth exploration of pupil behavior reflecting each attachment pattern, see Geddes, 2006, p. 67 onwards)

FRAMEWORK 4
PLAY DEVELOPMENT

Some of the children in our classrooms will not have learned the social and emotional skills which secure young children acquire through play. If they've lived in situations such as those described in the previous frameworks, they may not have had opportunity to develop their play-skills either. The development of play-skills is important, since waiting, taking turns, making mistakes, accepting rules, accepting others into our game and so on, are all vital for successful classroom learning.

If we consider for a moment how a young child learns to play, we can recognise the developmental stages cited by Winnicott (1971):

- Playing with the mother, not separate
- Playing with self, toes, fingers and so on
- Playing with an object, for example, a blanket, a soft toy
- Playing alone, but in the mother's presence
- Playing alongside another child (a stage often seen in nursery school, where two children will be playing, for example, in the 'home' area, but not with each other, alongside each other)
- Inviting another child to join in your play
- Being invited in to play another child's game and being able to follow their rules and inventions

It should be clear that for children to learn in our classrooms, we expect them to have reached Winnicott's last stage of play development, playing by someone else's rules. Some of the children we teach won't have reached this stage of play. They are unable to share the space between adult and child and make use of it for learning. In addition, we can identify a further stage of play development, not specifically mentioned by Winnicott, that of

- being able to negotiate the rules and procedure of play with another child so that a shared agreement is reached.

The lack of play-skills may show up in class as:

- ☐ being unable to take turns in class or in their group
- ☐ spoiling things for others, for example by cheating when they are not winning
- ☐ insisting on going first in games and sulking or getting angry if they are not picked
- ☐ trying to take over in group work with their peers and not listening to other people's ideas
- ☐ refusing to participate if the group overrides their decisions, or does not choose their ideas
- ☐ arguing about rules and instructions and then trying to change them if they're losing or getting something wrong, saying, for example, *"Well, when I did it before, we didn't do it like this"*

Some of the strategies proposed in this book are based on recognising what stage of play a child has reached and then developing appropriate tasks - both to ensure they engage in learning in our classrooms, and to help them develop the skills to progress to the next stage.

See *Chapters 2 and 6* for children who are unable to play alone, separate from the adult.
  Chapter 7 for a child unable to share the space and play alongside
  Chapter 4 for a child unable to invite others into his play
  Chapters 3 and 5 for children unable to play by others' rules
  Chapter 8 for a child unable to negotiate

Chapter 2

"What can I do with the kid who… continually calls out?"

Ms Jones is a caring teacher who tries hard to keep up with the latest teaching and learning ideas. She has been teaching English at a challenging secondary school for five years and generally has good relationships with her students. She is usually very patient with pupils with additional educational needs, but Lee, in her Year 7 class, is trying her patience and exhausting her energy. She says,

> "Lee never seems to settle to his work. He's always interrupting me, calling out "Miss, Miss, Miss", even when I've just told him to wait his turn or put his hand up. He doesn't seem to listen to any instructions, just asks me continually to come over and repeat them for him, as if he needs his own private lesson. Others in the class are fed up with him. He has a Teaching Assistant who gives him a lot of extra help and time in class. I seem to get drawn into spending ages with him too, as I can sense he's very needy. I even have to cut my lunch break short on occasion, as he's outside the staffroom looking for me. I sometimes pretend I'm not there, and ask another staff member to tell him to go away. Then I feel guilty, but I just can't spend all my time giving him extra special attention.
>
> And I get angry with him, he can be devious and manipulative. When he doesn't get his own way, he sulks or throws a tantrum. He always wants the Teaching Assistant to sit with him, and gets upset if she's working with

another child. When he does have her attention, she ends up doing most of the work for him, otherwise he'd never get started. I really don't think he is a bad boy, but I'm getting to the end of my tether with him"

Using the RETHINK model for thinking about Lee

We can see from the above description that Lee's behaviour is seriously frustrating for the teacher, and is getting in the way of the teaching and learning process. This type of constant, low-level, interrupting behaviour can be very wearing and time-consuming for a teacher to deal with. It spoils the flow of the class, and makes it difficult for other pupils to learn. We can use the **RETHINK** approach, described in Chapter 1, to try to understand what's happening in the classroom, to gain extra insight into the behaviour of the pupil and its impact on the teacher. We can then develop a set of strategies which should cut down on the teacher's frustration, save her time in the longer term, and allow her to focus once again on helping her class to learn.

STAGE 1   *REVIEW*

Review what is happening in class at the moment

We can **review** what is currently happening in the classroom interaction between Lee and Ms Jones, by imagining we are watching video footage of the lesson and can really focus on the detail. For example, what happens to Lee when he behaves inappropriately, calling out and seeking the teacher's attention all the time? Moreover, what happens to him when he behaves appropriately? What happens, for example, when he puts his hand up and waits to be noticed?

Perhaps he manages to attract and keep a lot of the teacher's attention when calling out inappropriately. Conversely, perhaps he is going *unnoticed* when he does the 'right' thing, and waits with his hand up. *What do we notice when we have the time and ability to step back and observe closely?*

Often, pupils such as Lee only get attention when they're calling out. We are so relieved when they're quiet that we forget to acknowledge them for behaving appropriately, or we decide they don't need praise for doing what's expected. But the message they can pick up is that we only notice bad behaviour.

We can **review** the classroom rules and check whether the pupil is really clear about them. Does he know the rule for asking questions? How do we know that this is clear to him? How is this reinforced during the lesson?

We can **review** the way instructions are given and how understanding is checked. Is the teacher giving clear verbal and visual instructions? Is there a demonstration of what is required? Is the pupil given an example and asked to provide one before starting the task? We can **review** our seating plan. Is Lee sitting in the right place to hear and see what's going on and not be disturbed by others?

These are all issues of classroom management. You can probably think of others to check your own clarity and consistency of rules *(and there are more ideas in the Checklist provided in Appendix A)*. If the teacher realises there are some general issues of class management, she might decide to **review** the rules with the whole class. At the same time, she could decide to say something specific to Lee to help him remember the rules 'in the moment', when he wants to call out something in class. The first set of stagies are based on these ideas.

REVIEW • RESPOND

Strategies

✔ Make it clear once again to Lee and the whole class that there are rules for speaking in class. However, resist the urge to correct Lee automatically during the lesson by saying *"Remember to put your hand up"*. It's more important to train Lee to trust his own brain and to learn to think alone, separate from the adult.

✔ You could say *"OK Lee, what rule are you breaking at the moment?"*

"How can you remember the right thing to do next time?"

"I wonder what you would need to think in order to stop yourself breaking this rule next time?"

✓ At the same time, make a mental note to notice when Lee is NOT calling out, and find a way to acknowledge this to him. For example, you might agree a signal such as a 'thumbs up', or have a piece of paper on his desk which you can put a tick on as you monitor the room.

STAGE 2 *REFRAME*

Reframe the behaviour

Simply training Lee to follow and remember the rules of the classroom might not be enough for a child who often behaves in this way. If you have tried some of the strategies above and the behaviour isn't decreasing, we need to think a bit more about what might be going on in the classroom for him. In order to do this, we need to be able to describe Lee's behaviour exactly and objectively, separating the precise description from our judgment of it. We can then **reframe** our interpretation of the behaviour in a more positive way.

Why should we describe and reframe?

With this type of pupil, we often sit round in the staffroom discussing their latest misdemeanors, with everyone agreeing that the child/adolescent is devious and manipulative. This might have a slightly cathartic effect for us, as we can vent our feelings; but, in general, it doesn't lead us to finding positive strategies for dealing with the child. If anything, we often feel worse and even guilty at expressing such strong negative feelings about the pupil. In the example above, the teacher is describing the situation with judgmental words. Words such as *"devious ... manipulative.."* are unhelpful, as they are our personal interpretations and mind-reading of the situation.

If we say to a child *"You are very manipulative",* we invite the child to become defensive and disagree with us, as much as we would if someone said it us. It becomes a *"Yes, you are!", "No I'm not!"* kind of conversation. Furthermore, these kinds of words can make it difficult to look at what is actually happening and think logically about it. By using this type of language to ourselves, we are automatically setting up a negative interaction.

Instead, let's **reframe** our language by asking ourselves, what exactly does he do that makes us feel we are being manipulated? What exactly is the behaviour that we are describing as devious? Once we are clear in our description of the exact behaviour, we can make sure we use this language when we are speaking to the pupil about the problem. For example, we can say;

"*When you call out at the same time as I'm presenting new information,*

(the specific behaviour and specific situation) *it makes it difficult for other*

people to hear what I am saying" (description of consequence).

We can also **reframe** by choosing to see a positive intention in the behaviour rather than judging it in a negative way. So, back in the staffroom or in our own reflection, we can ask, *"What might be the positive intention driving this behaviour?"*

For example, we could choose to believe that Lee is calling out because he thinks the teacher is the most important person in the room, and wants to show her that he has recognised her vital role. You might think of another positive intention. What matters is that we find an intention which we *genuinely believe* to be positive. Many teachers at this stage would say that Lee's behaviour is attention-seeking, but, in my experience, we rarely say this in an empathic or appreciative way about a child in our class. We'll need to stretch our imaginations to come up with positive intentions, which may feel uncomfortable and unnatural at first. If it were easy, we wouldn't find the behaviour so challenging!

The second bank of strategies is based on how we might use the information we gather from this type of describing and **reframing.**

REFRAME • RESPOND

Strategies

✔ Reframe the behaviour which is annoying you and describe your interpretation to the pupil, for example:

"When you shout out in the middle of my explanation, I think that means you're not listening properly"

✔ Reframe this description of behaviour by thinking of a possible positive intention to the behaviour and naming this. *You* might decide that Lee's positive intention, in the example given above, is to show the teacher how much he knows. In this case, you could say:

"It's great that you want to show how much you know, and I need you to remember the rule about putting your hand up"

✔ Reframe the behaviour as a learning opportunity. You might decide that the inappropriate behaviour presents an opportunity to help Lee learn to manage himself better. You could see it as an interesting, positive interaction, and chance to put the control back within the child. You might choose to say:

"Lee, how can you stop yourself calling out… what would help you to stop calling out…?"

"What would you need to believe or have to stop doing this?"

"How can I support you with that?"

It's important to work with the answers which come from the child, and not try to impose our own answers. For example, in reply to the above questions, Alison, 13, said:

"I need to believe that you still like me, because when you're over there, it's as if you are ignoring me. Can you just show me that you aren't?" Her teacher asked, *"How would you want me to show you?"*. Alison suggested,

"Just look over and maybe hold your hand up to show how many minutes before you come back".

STAGE 3 *REFLECT*

Reflect on the pupil's needs and feelings

With some students, the strategies and comments outlined above may be enough for them to learn the required behaviour. However, if the behaviour persists, it may be showing us that this student has some unmet need which is driving the classroom behaviour.

We then have to consider those three key questions from Chapter 1:

> **What is the UNMET NEED the child is trying to fulfill through this behaviour?**
>
> **What has this child NOT had experience of?**
>
> **What is it that this child CANNOT believe about the teacher and the classroom?**

Let's look at what Lee appears to need. He seems to be unable to focus on the task. He is constantly checking whether the teacher has noticed him, in other words, whether the teacher is *keeping him in mind*. It could be that Lee is an example of a child who, for whatever reasons, has not learned to believe that the teacher will remember him unless he is continually calling out. He has had, in Bion's terms (1962), no experience of being 'held in mind'. His continual need to check out the relationship with the teacher means that he isn't getting down to the task. Perhaps he hasn't had the opportunity to develop a secure sense of self which is separate from the person supposed to be caring for him. He needs a thinking adult to help him to do this. By appearing more helpless than he actually is, he's found a way of maintaining the connection with the adult.

If we view Lee's behaviour in this way, we can develop the following list of his needs:

- to have an experience of being thought about and remembered
- to have his sense of anxiety 'contained' (p.70) so that he can realise the world will not fall apart if he separates from the relationship
- to trust that the relationship is still there if he gets on with the task
- to know how to attract attention appropriately
- to recognise that the teacher will be able give him attention at an appropriate time
- to learn how to wait, and to know how long he's been waiting
- to bear the frustration of not knowing if he'll be remembered
- to develop a sense of his own thinking brain, separate to the adult, and trust his own thoughts without the teacher or another adult rushing in to help too soon
- to know that if the teacher spends longer with another pupil, it is not a deliberate forgetting of him or the end of the world

FRAMEWORK I WHERE THE FEELINGS COME FROM

If we look at the feelings which the staff have in relation to Lee, we can see that there is a sense of:

→   wanting to help
→   recognising he needs a lot of special attention
→   feeling that no amount of attention ever seems to be enough for Lee
→   feeling exasperated and manipulated by him
→   feeling guilty for getting frustrated and angry with him

These feelings might be evidence that there is an unconscious defence mechanism in operation in this classroom - that of *transference*. Ms Jones and her TA find themselves caught up in a pattern of behaviour with Lee that may be a replication of his early relationship with a parent or carer. At times, they are replaying the inconsistency of his early years - sometimes giving Lee lots of help, even over-helping, and at other times pulling away from him and rejecting his demands. All the strategies suggested below involve the teacher being able to spot this pattern and trying to do something to break it, thus not getting caught up in the *counter-transference*.

FRAMEWORK 2 THE EFFECTS OF TRAUMA ON LEARNING
Why Lee might not be able to learn

As a classroom teacher, Ms Jones might not know much about Lee's background. However, if we think about the effects of specific traumatic circumstances on learning (*as described on pp.23-6*), we might gain some added insight into Lee's behaviour. We might be curious about what has happened to bring Lee to a point where he can't believe an adult will remember him when he's out of their sight. This might have happened as a result of his parent or carer providing an inconsistent response to his early needs. Inconsistent parental responses can be caused by many factors. For example, Lee might have had a parent who was suffering from drug or alcohol addiction. At times, this parent might have been able to parent Lee in a loving and predictable way, but at other times, may have been too 'out of it' to respond consistently. Children in care who've experienced multiple moves back and forth from parental home to foster care, may have also had very inconsistent parenting. So these children will have learned that they can't trust an adult to remember them, and will be constantly checking out the relationship with the teacher.

Access to such information can contribute to the teacher and other staff developing an understanding of Lee's behaviour in class. We might want to ask why he has learned to manipulate adults and what purpose this served for him or protected him from. It would not generally be appropriate to comment on this in our dealing with the child, but we should bear it in mind when we think about his needs and how we name and deal with his anxieties in the classroom.

FRAMEWORK 3 ATTACHMENT PATTERN

In terms of attachment patterns, the needs we have identified above might suggest Lee is exhibiting a behaviour pattern indicative of *insecure/ambivalent-resistant* attachment (*see p.28*), as he needs to continually check the relationship with the adult, *to the detriment of his ability to concentrate on the task.* This often means that he takes an excessively long time to start any task, and as a consequence, rarely completes a piece of work.

FRAMEWORK 4 PLAY DEVELOPMENT

In terms of play, Lee seems to be unable to separate from the adult and play by himself. For learning to take place, he needs a sense of separation, and being able to exist on his own with the activity. This is similar to a small child needing to learn that it is safe to play on their own with their toys, even when their carer is not directly talking to them or playing with them – that the carer is still *'holding them in mind'*, and has not forgotten about them.

By taking some time to reflect on Lee's needs as outlined above within the four frameworks, we can use what we have identified to develop concrete teaching strategies, those which we can address in our lesson planning: those which we can use in the classroom as 'on-the-spot' responses: and, where possible, those which can be applied outside the classroom, around the school.

REFLECTION • RESPOND

Strategies

I   LESSON PLANNING

Lesson planning will be driven by bearing in mind what Lee needs from us as a teacher in the moment, and the skills he needs to develop in order to engage successfully in the learning process. So we may decide, for example to:

✔ Set small timed tasks which gradually wean Lee away from dependence on the teacher's presence, but allow him to learn to trust that you will not forget about him. This can be marked with younger children with egg-timers, and older pupils with the clock-face or their own watch

✔ Choose tasks which follow a known pattern and are easy to start, so there can be no disagreements about not being able to do it. For example, you might start each task with a review of key words in the form of a word scramble

✔ Think about what Lee cannot do and, wherever possible, devise activities which practise these skills. This is anyway likely to be beneficial for the whole class. Lee doesn't seem to be able to wait for any length of time for the teacher's attention: in other words, he finds it hard to measure time. So you might include the warm-up activity of *"How long is a minute?"*

⏲ **ACTIVITY**   **How long is a minute?**   (**warm-up**)

Students stand up in front of their chairs and close their eyes. When the teacher says *"Go"*, the students must measure a minute in their minds and sit down when they think a minute has gone by. When everyone has sat down, the teacher gives feedback on how near to a minute they were. Pupils who are successful should share their strategies with the group and the class should try again. Children such as Lee often sit down after just a few seconds, as time seems very long for them. This activity teaches them, as well as the rest of the class, how to measure time more realistically.

✋ ACTIVITY Counting to 10 to leave the class (finishing the lesson)

At the end of the lesson, the class has to count to ten. Only one person can speak at a time, and there can be no discussion on how to do this. One pupil starts, and says "One". Any pupil can continue and say "Two" and then another pupil should say "Three" and so on. If two pupils speak at once, the class has to start again. In order to play this game, pupils have to wait and listen to each other, and work as a team. For pupils such as Lee, this is a challenge, as they will want to call out all the time. Making it a team game can help them learn to manage this better. The basic idea of this activity can be adapted according to subject; for example, in a foreign language lesson, the pupils say the numbers in the language being taught, or in maths, they could count upwards in an agreed number pattern, such as x+1.

II   PLANNING 'ON THE SPOT' RESPONSES

✔ It isn't always possible to build in activities which develop the skills the pupil has shown they need to learn. You can, however, decide what you are going to say in response to the specific unmet needs that you think Lee has, as identified in your reflection. So you might choose to say:
"Try the first 3 questions on your own and then I'll come back and check"

✔ Make sure you do go back, and, if you get distracted, that you acknowledge what has happened:
"I am sorry I didn't get back to you when we agreed, that must have been worrying for you. You probably thought I'd forgotten you, but I hadn't"

✔ Avoid the temptation to over-help. These children need to experience some frustration in order to develop their ability to problem-solve and learn. You can acknowledge their frustration:

"I know it can feel impossible to do this work without the teacher next to you. It can feel very frustrating when we are learning something new. You can trust your brain to do it though".

✔ For example, this pupil might continually be asking

"How do you spell that?"

Avoid the urge to answer immediately or rebuff: both are examples of not giving the child an experience of being confused and risking thinking through the frustration. Say instead:

"Trust your own brain. What does it think?"

✔ Name the anxiety they might be feeling when you have left them to attend to the needs of another student or students:

"I know you find it hard to believe that I'll remember you when I'm not speaking to you on your own"

"Maybe it's hard to believe that I haven't forgotten you when I'm talking to the whole class, but I haven't"

✔ Show Lee that he is remembered at other times. This can be done by mentioning something which shows you were thinking about him outside the class. For example, if you know what football team he supports, you might say:

"I see Arsenal had a hard match on Saturday. I wondered if you watched it"

✔ Or comment on a general interest that may link Lee to others in the class:

"I was in a shop at the weekend and I saw that the new DS game is out, the one you were talking about last week"

✔ Or, if you don't know much personal information about Lee, you could show you remember him from your previous class:

"Last class Lee made an interesting point about the main character in this book"

III   PLANNING FOR OUTSIDE CLASS TIME

The needs identified earlier might lead you to make a plan for Lee outside class time.

- ✔ If you acknowledge that Lee needs some way to keep contact with a teacher, you could arrange to let him help once a week with something at lunchtime. It would be important to make sure that Lee knows the exact day and time. Without this, he is likely to come on other days, and ask if he can help at other times. It needs to be made clear to him that he has a set time and that that's the time to come. You can help him to manage this anxiety (about being forgotten) by referring to your meetings at other times. For example, you might say after class:
  "I'm really pleased you are going to help me to sort that cupboard out on Tuesday lunchtime. I need help with that".

- ✔ Make sure the time spent together is positive and something to look forward to. The example above, of sorting out a cupboard, does not need to be a 'chore', it can be a shared, productive experience which gives the opportunity for some informal chat and interaction. By letting the child know that he is genuinely needed and that his help is valued, the time together will become more important and satisfying for him than time he used to get by manipulation.

- ✔ Maintaining this clear timetable for meetings will help Lee to gradually separate from the teacher, enjoy the time they do spend together, and trust he won't be forgotten by her the rest of the week.

- ✔ You could also help Lee to develop relationships with his peers, and move away from the constant checking with the teacher, by allocating a peer mentor or older student to get him involved in a club

In conclusion

There are no quick and easy answers to dealing with a behaviour which has been learned over time. However, if you follow the **RETHINK** approach, you should see some improvement in the pupil's behaviour. You can't expect the pupil to become 'perfect' and never again call out inappropriately, but:

You'll know that a kid who constantly calls out is making progress when ...

★ he can start his work, most of the time, immediately after you've explained what to do to the whole class

★ the amount of time you spend re-explaining the task to him individually is reduced

★ he can share Teaching Assistant time with another pupil

★ he can keep to set appointments to meet with you and doesn't turn up outside these times, saying he "forgot"

★ he leaves the classroom at the end of the lesson or at breaks without lingering on too long

★ you don't feel he's using up your goodwill and energy whenever you interact with him. Instead, you begin to find you can enjoy your conversations

★ he can meet you in the corridor, say "Hi Miss", and keep on walking!

Chapter 3

"What can I do with the kid who... rubbishes their work and the teacher?"

Jamie is a year 6 pupil and her class teacher is very worried about her. She says that she has yet to get a piece of work handed in and completed by this pupil. Jamie often starts well, working independently and neatly, but at some stage gets frustrated and tears her work up or crosses everything out. She refuses help and gets angry and abusive to the teacher or Teaching Assistant who are trying to reassure her that her work is good. Her teacher also says,

> "I find myself getting very angry with Jamie. I feel useless as a teacher, and I almost want to grab the task out of her hands before she can rip it up. She makes me feel completely powerless. She was assigned a Teaching Assistant as we thought maybe some positive attention and encouragement would help her get the work done, but Jamie refuses help from her, saying that she hates her. At the end of last term, she was successful in a reading competition and was presented with an award. She refused to go up in assembly and collect it, and wouldn't have her photo taken either. Then she threw the certificate away. Praise doesn't seem to work with Jamie. Her mother came to the awards ceremony and was very upset that she behaved so badly."

Using the RETHINK model for thinking about Jamie

We can see from the above description that Jamie's behaviour is causing concern and anger for her teacher as well as for her mother. Her own frustration is getting in the way of her learning and even her ability to enjoy potentially positive school experiences, such as awards assemblies. We can use the **RETHINK** approach, described in Chapter 1, to try to understand what is happening in the classroom for Jamie and her teacher.

STAGE 1   *REVIEW*

Review what is happening in class at the moment

We can begin by reviewing what is currently happening in the classroom. The teacher could choose to review her classroom management and lesson planning to look at how these factors are currently impacting on Jamie.

Classroom management

Are the rules for getting help clear to Jamie? How does the teacher know this, and is it constantly clarified for pupils? For example, if there is a rule for putting your hand up to ask for help, is it consistently applied or do some pupils wait without getting noticed, whilst others get attention by calling out? Do other pupils ask for help when they're stuck, or would Jamie be the only one drawing attention to herself in this way? Is the work at an appropriate level for Jamie, or is she getting frustrated and tearing it up because it's too easy or too difficult for her? Is there a clear and consistent reward system so that when pupils get a reward, they know what it's for and the reward is meaningful to them? Has the role of the Teaching Assistant been made clear? Does the TA work with groups of pupils, or only a few with learning difficulties? Could it be this which is influencing Jamie's reluctance to work with her?

All of these are classroom management and planning issues, which would need to be reviewed before moving on to looking at other factors which might be underlying Jamie's behaviour.

Staff responses to Jamie's behaviour

Let's assume that this teacher has good classroom management skills and the rules are clear to pupils. So now let's look in detail at Jamie's interaction with staff and **review** the pattern of staff response to Jamie's behaviour. What reaction does Jamie get *in the moment?*

Essentially the reaction is one of reassurance. The staff try to verbally reassure Jamie that her work is good, and try to stop her destroying it. They're using public praise and rewards. They're telling Jamie that she's doing well. They're trying to build a positive relationship with her, which are all strategies of good, positive behaviour management. But in effect, by carrying out their wish to pass something positive (praise and reassurance) from them to the child, they are doing more of what this child appears not able to do - they are 'doing' more of the relationship.

Jamie's behaviour would suggest that she isn't used to praise and rewards. Being noticed, even in a positive way, appears to upset her, and provokes a very strong negative reaction. Direct relationship-making doesn't appear to be working: so we need to **review** our responses, and maybe do something different.

REVIEW • RESPOND

Strategies

- ✓ Stop trying to make a direct relationship with Jamie. If something isn't working, don't do more of it: do something different
- ✓ Reassurance isn't working either. Try simply naming what is happening. You might say: *"You want to do it perfectly and get upset/annoyed when it is not to your standard"*
  "You want to do it on your own, without our help"

"What do you think we can do to get this finished?"

✔ Notice when Jamie is engaged, and use these kinds of tasks.

You can then comment on the tasks using impersonal language.

For example:

"Number 3 is a bit more difficult. There is an example on the board".

This is different to *"I see you have found number 3 a bit difficult. Let me show you another example on the board"*

Saying *"**I** see"* and *"Let **me**"* suggests that you are important in the interaction, and children like Jamie find it really difficult to cope with this

✔ Notice if Jamie can work with any other students. Sit her with them

✔ Give praise differently. Maybe Jamie can accept praise in a letter home, or a private word, or a tick on her book. She may need to learn to accept certificates in private in an envelope before she can accept anything in public. You could try just leaving them in her tray with a message

✔ Find imaginative ways to acknowledge her work in public.

For example, you might take a picture of it or scan it for a newsletter or wall display

✔ Tackle the issue of not finishing work and tearing it up by asking the child:

"How can we put this to one side for the moment., and not completely throw it away?"

✔ Sometimes it can help to suggest that work is stored in a temporary box or carton, and then reviewed after a period of time to see if it can be kept, worked on or thrown away. The storage could be an A4 box folder or something similar. Set up a system of looking at the work at the end of the week to decide what to do with it (*this idea came from a child who was asked the above question*)

STAGE 2 **REFRAME**

Interpretations

In order to **reframe** how the teacher understands Jamie's behaviour, we need to separate out the *description* of the behaviour from how the teacher interprets it and how it makes her feel. She might say:

DESCRIPTION	INTERPRETATIONS AND FEELINGS
"When Jamie sits on her own, turns away from me and puts her hand over her work,	… it makes me **think** she is rejecting my help and I **feel** quite incompetent when I am near her
When I then come over to her and ask her if everything is alright and she puts her head down, says nothing in reply but just rips up her work,	… it makes me **think** she doesn't trust me and I **feel** useless and redundant:
When I'm walking around the room and I say to her as a I walk past that she is working well, and she looks away or scribbles on her work,	… I **feel** completely powerless and ineffective, and it makes me **think** she doesn't even like me".

So in order not to confuse our own reactions with what Jamie is actually doing, we need to separate out what can be observed from our interpretations and feelings.

We will then be able to decide on strategies which address the specific behaviour.

The most striking thing to notice in the description above was the *intensity* of the teacher's feelings. We can name these feelings and **reframe** their meaning to give us important information about what might be going on for Jamie. The teacher is experiencing:

→   a feeling of not being allowed to teach, of being redundant: perhaps we could **reframe** this as a sign that Jamie, for whatever reason, can't bear to let the teacher have the power of knowing more than her

→   a feeling of uselessness and powerlessness: perhaps we could **reframe** this as information about how Jamie might be feeling in class

(*for more on this, see projection below*)

We can also **reframe** what being noticed seems to mean to Jamie. For example, Jamie and other children like her may experience praise as persecutory, or as a forerunner to possible humiliation. **Reframe** their negative reaction to praise by considering; if you yourself only knew denigration and failure, how might you deal with success, completion and moving on? Might you not interpret 'success' as a warning that humiliation will follow? There is a key point to remember - some of the most successful principles of good behaviour management do not work with children who have not learned to trust success and praise.

Thus we can **reframe** Jamie's apparent indifference to the teacher and to praise as a desire to be independent, and as a way of keeping herself safe from a potentially dangerous relationship.

REFRAME • RESPOND
Strategies

✔   Notice your own feelings and use these as information about how the child might be feeling

✔ Find ways to give verbal praise which allow the child to keep herself safe. For example, say,

"*You must be proud of yourself*" rather than "***I** am proud of you*"

STAGE 3 *REFLECT*

Reflect on the pupil's needs and feelings

With some students, the strategies and insights from the **review** and **reframe** stages might be enough to help the teacher to manage the behaviour better. However, if Jamie's behaviour persists, we need to think a bit more about what might be driving it. The child may be showing us an unmet need which is underlying her actions in class. We then have to consider those three key questions from Chapter 1:

What is the UNMET NEED the child is trying to fulfill through this behaviour?

What has this child NOT had experience of?

What is it that this child CANNOT believe about the teacher and the classroom?

FRAMEWORK I WHERE THE FEELINGS COME FROM

We can use the information about the teacher's feelings to understand Jamie's deeper needs. The teacher is experiencing a feeling of 'not being allowed to teach', feelings of uselessness and powerlessness. This could be an example of the unconscious defence mechanism of *projection*.

Projection occurs when we have unbearably painful feelings and we unconsciously externalise them, 'pushing them out' and trying to attribute them to others. We cannot bear to think about them and therefore unconsciously 'look' for another person to 'hold' the feelings, to experience them and take them away from us. While we cannot know for sure, the teacher's feelings of hopelessness and uselessness might well be an indication of how Jamie is feeling. We can use this feeling to guide our planning.

We also need to consider Jamie's explict feelings. Jamie appears to be feeling very angry and showing this in her negative reaction to offers of help and in tearing up her work. This might be an example of *displacement,* another type of defence mechanism. Displacement happens when an emotion we are feeling about a particular relationship or person in our life cannot be safely expressed toward that person, but is directed instead toward another person or into another situation. If we think about Jamie's feelings in this way, we might wonder who the young person is angry with and where that strength of feeling came from originally. We can see that Jamie needs to:

- keep control of the situation, so that the teacher will not have the power to hurt her or make her feel powerless by knowing something better than she does
- manage the task without admitting to the adult that she needs help. Asking for help would mean trusting the relationship with the teacher, and this can feel dangerous for children such as Jamie
- keep herself safe from possible humiliation and feeling stupid
- be able to learn to make use of the relationship with the teacher to progress her learning, because at the moment whilst she's doing quite well, she won't realise her full potential without accepting help
- learn to accept positive affirmations, so that she can develop a more positive, less fragile sense of self

When developing strategies to deal with Jamie's behaviour, we need to make sure we include those which can address these needs. Before we do this, it can be helpful to think about what has brought Jamie to this place. What might have happened to shape her responses to adults in the ways described above?

FRAMEWORK 2 THE EFFECTS OF TRAUMA ON LEARNING

As a classroom teacher, you might not know much about the background of a child such as Jamie, but her behaviour might give you some insights into what her experience of adults has been. She has somehow learned that asking for help isn't a good thing and that adults can't be trusted to respond appropriately. She may have lived or be living in violent circumstances, or have experienced severe loss or separation, the experience of adults 'not being there for her' (*see p.25 for more detailed discussion*). By recognising the effect of trauma on the key learning skill of being able to ask for help, we can begin to think about ways of giving Jamie the experience she hasn't had - the experience of an available adult who can offer help without it being humiliating. Jamie can't believe that such an adult exists, or that asking for help will lead to anything other than denigration. We need to understand that Jamie's needs can't be met simply by offering more help in a more caring way. Why should this be trusted by a child like Jamie?

FRAMEWORK 3 ATTACHMENT PATTERN

Jamie appears to be exhibiting an *insecure/avoidant* attachment pattern. If we think about what this means (*see p.28*), we will see that developing a relationship through the task is the safe way forward for this child. Jamie needs to be able to become comfortable with making use of the relationship to progress her learning, but this needs to happen through a step-by-step approach through careful planning and appropriate tasks.

FRAMEWORK 4 PLAY DEVELOPMENT

Jamie cannot let others play unless they play completely by her rules. She has not reached the stage of being able to turn-take, and cannot bear to relinquish control in case a catastrophe occurs (such as the opportunity to take part being snatched away from her forever, or the adult getting angry and stopping the game for no apparent reason). These are all experiences which Jamie may have had and which will make it difficult for her to believe the school experience will be different. So she needs some activities which allow her to work alongside others. These will enable her to learn to move along the play continuum, and begin to share the learning space with the other pupils and the teacher.

REFLECT • RESPOND

Strategies

I   LESSON PLANNING

It is vital to remember that the 'Jamies' in our classrooms are able to deal with the task but not the relationship.

✔ Plan tasks which allow Jamie to work alongside another child or adult and work indirectly

✔ Decide to build in some choice in the work where possible:
"*We need to learn these words. You can choose to do the word search first, or start with the matching exercise*"

✔ Organise group work with different roles and information.
This type of child often responds to having a clear role and responsibility in a group of peers. Having a role in a smaller group can make the interactions feel safer, as the child can focus on the task element of their role and does not have to engage directly in a relationship with teacher. They might, for example, research some information for a presentation, and other pupils can present the findings to the teacher and the class. Doing research can feel easier and safer for a child such as Jamie, as it is a more open-ended, exploratory task which does not have an obvious right and wrong answer in the way that most classroom tasks do: the child's desire to work independently can be seen as a strength rather than a weakness.

✔ Plan games and activities with an element of competition, so that Jamie can practise losing: but be prepared to name the anxiety:

"It can feel unbearable to lose ... it can be hard to lose and that's OK"

✔ Invent games where the aim is to lose - you win by losing!

♣ ACTIVITY Try not to win! (cooperative group activity)

In groups, ask pupils to think of a game they like playing. This is often done best with a card game. Then ask each group to write a simple set of rules for the game. Let them play the game once in the normal way. Now ask them to give the instructions for their game to a different group.

Now tell each group that they need to re-write the instructions for the game they have received, by reversing all the rules. For example, if you usually have to get rid of all your cards, this time you have to try to keep as many as possible. If you normally have to be the fastest player, you have to try to be the slowest player. Let them play the game in their group with the new rules.

Usually groups become quite confused, but find the game enjoyable.

Over time this blurs the lines between winning and losing for children like Jamie, gradually allowing them to come to simply enjoy playing.

II   PLANNING WHAT TO SAY 'ON THE SPOT'

Things to say to ourselves

✔ If we think our feeling of uselessness is an example of projection, we might reframe it as important information about how the *child* may be feeling

✔ If we think such feelings are an example of displacement, we might say to ourselves *"This is not meant for me"* (it can be a relief to realise the situation is not all our fault) - and - *"I wonder who this pupil is really angry at?"*

Things to say to the child

✔ If it seems appropriate, name the projection.

For example, you might say:

"*I feel a bit stuck now, perhaps that's how you feel?*" "*Sometimes when we're learning, we can all feel a bit useless if we can't do something in the way we want*"

✔ Instead of reassuring the pupil about being 'good-enough', name the anxiety about being not being perfect: "*You can't bear to get it wrong or less than perfect. It is possible for something to be good and also need some improvement*" "*Not knowing something can feel terrible*"

✔ Acknowledge how hard it is for the child to change her beliefs about herself: "*You find it hard to believe this is good enough*"

✔ The skill she needs to learn is to allow some imperfection or middle ground between perfect and useless. Use any opportunities to show that everyone makes mistakes and can learn from them. Wherever possible, include your own examples of learning through making mistakes. You also need to model this, so if you get something wrong, admit it, or wonder with the class how to do something better

✔ Eventually, the child needs to learn to make use of the relationship with the teaching staff, so that she can make real progress with the task. In this way, she is far more likely to maximise her true learning potential: "*You have nearly finished that on your own, and perhaps Ms A can now look at it with you.*"

III   PLANNING FOR OUTSIDE CLASS TIME

✔ Find out if the child has any special abilities or interests and find ways to encourage Jamie to share these with other pupils and staff. She needs to learn that relationships in general can be safe. This type of child can often become very involved in a particular hobby or interest which they are probably pursuing on their own. For example, you may find that they are very good at chess, but there is no chess club in school - maybe ask them to help another pupil to set it up

✔ If your school has peer mentors or educators, try to match Jamie with someone with a similar interest. The relationship will develop through the shared interest, not interpersonally to begin with

✔ Exploit opportunities to become involved in drama and film - this type of child can often engage in the storylines of a production or film club, because the feelings and relationships are explored indirectly, through the metaphor of acting. They are unlikely to want to be involved in rehearsals and performance, but will often have good ideas for plot or characters

✔ If there is an opportunity for this child to work in a small group with Learning Mentors or Teaching Assistants, include activities such as the Squiggle game, shared storywriting and board games to practice the skills of sharing a space with others

🖉 ACTIVITY The squiggle game   (warm up)

Pupils play in pairs. One person closes their eyes and draws a squiggle on the paper. Their partner looks at the squiggle and tries to make it into a picture of something. Emphasise that there are no right or wrong answers. The pairs then swap roles and do the activity again. Let them have three or more goes each. This is a good game to help children like Jamie share the learning space with someone else, without fear that there is someone who has more knowledge than the other. You can extend this activity by asking pupils to make up a story based on their picture squiggles, or you can simply use the activity as a creative warm up-activity. As you do it more often, the child usually becomes freer in their thinking and their creativity.

(This activity was used extensively by Winnicott in his play therapy. See Winnicott, 1971)
For other good ideas, see the Anti-Colouring Book, Striker, 2004)

You'll know a kid who rips up work is making progress when …

★ she can hand in work which isn't completely finished or is less than perfect

★ she asks you or a TA for help

★ she has joined in other aspects of school life or an outside club

★ she show you in some way that she has noticed something about you (although the comment might not necessarily be positive!). For example, she might ask you why you got your hair cut, in a tone that implies it was a mistake!

★ she sometimes chooses to sit with other pupils rather than at the back of the class on her own

★ she can manage her upset about getting something wrong. She might still stop working and look upset, or rub or cross out work furiously, but she can begin again after a calming down period

★ she can have a laugh about losing in a game!

Chapter 4

"What can I do with the kid who… is too quiet and withdrawn?"

We should remember that is not always the pupils who 'act out' that cause us concern.

John is a pupil in year 8, who always sits near the front of the class on his own. His form teacher says:

> "John always seems to look sad. He comes into class without a word, takes out his books when asked, and usually follows all of my instructions. He's compliant, but never offers any answers, and he sometimes seems unable to respond when I ask him a direct question. I feel completely helpless, as I want to help him, but I can't seem to get through to him. At times he seems oblivious to me and the rest of the class. I've tried asking him if he is OK and trying to find out more about his interests, but he just keeps his head down and mutters that everything is fine. I want to spend more time speaking to him and getting to know him, but inevitably my time gets taken up by someone else who is louder or more attention-seeking".

Using the RETHINK model for thinking about John

We can see from the above description that John's behaviour isn't causing any immediately observable problems in the classroom. It doesn't interfere with other pupil's learning or the teacher's ability to teach the class. However, we can use the **RETHINK** model to explore the teacher's feeling that all is not well with John. Pupils who are withdrawn and overly quiet can be a challenge to teach, because we can suddenly realise that they're not making the progress we expected, and that we hadn't noticed they were slipping behind. It's as if they are invisible, remaining 'under our radar'.

STAGE 1 *REVIEW*

Review what is happening in class at the moment

There would appear to be no classroom management or behaviour issues with a child like John. He doesn't demand extra time, he completes his work, he obeys classroom rules. But there are many other aspects of what's happening that we can **review**, to find a way forward.

To begin with, this type of child often gets overlooked: teachers sometimes even have trouble remembering their names. As a colleague of John's teacher says,

> *"When you asked me what I thought of John's behaviour, I thought "John who"? And then I wondered why you thought it was a problem. I have far more pressing concerns than a pupil who just gets on with his work and is maybe just a bit shy".*

However, the form teacher is feeling concerned. Something doesn't feel right. As teachers, it's always useful to take some time to think about any 'gut' feelings you have about a child. In John's case, we can **review** his behaviour in terms of what he is NOT doing, and we might see some areas of concern.

John's behaviour

Let's look at his behaviour in detail. John doesn't make eye contact, and he keeps his head down when he's spoken to. This leads the teacher to feel there is no communication. When the teacher is asked to describe what John does more specifically, she says:

"He often sits on his own and doesn't speak to the other pupils. When I ask him a question, he can't answer immediately, looks around or at the table and his face becomes quite tense. When he comes into class, he usually doesn't say hello to anyone, but quietly sits down and starts searching in his bag for things. When he's got all his equipment out, he spends time lining it all up and making it orderly. I notice sometimes he seems to concentrate really intensely on small tasks, gripping the ruler so tightly his knuckles are white."

This detailed description of John's behaviour is helpful, as it illustrates why the teacher really might have reason for concern, particularly in relation to John's apparent lack of social interaction and distraction from the task.

How others respond to John in class

We could also take the time to observe the teacher's responses in detail. What happens when John doesn't answer a direct question? Is he left alone and not asked again? What happens when he doesn't make eye contact? Does the teacher insist that he looks at her? Does he then do it, and in what way? We might want a pupil to make eye contact to show they are listening, understanding and interacting, but forcing him to do this might have the opposite effect. How do the other pupils react to John? Do they ask him to sit near them, do they choose to sit with him, or do they avoid him? Often, pupils such as John can exist in a classroom as a small, quiet island, around which interaction takes place but which passes over them. By developing our ability to observe the small details of classroom interaction, we can ensure that all the children in our classes, even these 'invisible' ones, are being included in our teaching.

Teaching/Learning styles

Finally, we can also **review** our own teaching and learning style, in order to assess how adequately we are addressing John's learning preferences. As teachers we tend to feel most comfortable with learners who fit a learning style we understand. It could be that John has a very different learning style to his teacher and that, for example, in Gardner's terms (1983,1993), he has more of an intrapersonal learning profile, preferring to think about things on his own rather than work in groups. His desire to keep things neat and orderly may be a sign that he has a logical-mathematical and visual learning preference.

Once we've **reviewed** these three elements, we can think what would be helpful for us as teachers to change. We might want to find ways to include John in the classroom and develop his social skills, without becoming too intrusive or focusing on him too directly.

REVIEW • RESPOND

Strategies

- ✔ Avoid insisting John makes eye contact with you. If this might be intrusive, insisting is even more so! Instead, try to use curriculum opportunities to indirectly support John to learn this core social skill. For example, use geography to discuss different cultures views of eye contact, use portraits in art and history to discuss why we think someone is feeling a certain way, and the importance of the eye in conveying feeling

- ✔ Put instructions on the board or projector so John has to look up in order to do the task rather than just because the teacher is forcing him to

- ✔ Use the board for memory games which involve looking up. For example, keywords which need to be remembered can be written on the board (such as important labels in a biology diagram): one word can then be deleted, and pupils have to say which one is missing

- ✔ Work with John's perceived learning style. This pupil might be quite visual, using colours, liking things neat, orderly. Written instructions rather than verbal ones can work well. He might need time to think about his answers, rather than being put on the spot in a group. He might prefer to draw and map out information before verbalising it.

STAGE 2 *REFRAME*

Reframe the behaviour

It might be that by **reviewing** our current classroom practice around John, we find ways to involve and include him more in our thinking. This could be enough to involve him more in the class and increase his social interaction. However, there might be other ways of looking at John's behaviour, and it might be necessary to **reframe** some of our thinking around this to help him further. The teacher says,

DESCRIPTION	INTERPRETATIONS AND FEELINGS
"When John does not make eye contact with me,	*... it makes me **wonder** if he finds someone looking at him too intrusive: I also **wonder** if this is a way to put other students off working with him*
When he continues to search for things in his bag whilst I'm talking to him,	*... I **feel** he's oblivious to me and extremely anxious about something"*

By making this distinction, the teacher is at least thinking about John and what his behaviour means. The problem with children like John is that we often don't think about them at all. We might fleetingly worry about them in class, but generally pupils who 'act out' or are more demanding of our attention take over our thoughts. If you want to consider such a child in your class, look at the list of pupils you have for a parents' evening: how many faces and personalities can you instantly recall? John will be one of those whose face might escape you and whose learning might be difficult to assess, because you'll suddenly realise you haven't noticed how he is progressing. We've all done it.

We could **reframe** John's seemingly compliant behaviour as avoiding any close or meaningful relationships with staff or peers. We could **reframe** his constant searching in his bag as an uncontained anxiety about being in the group (*by uncontained, I mean that John may not have had an experience of a caring adult recognising his feelings, trying to understand and name his anxiety, and if appropriate, talk with him about it in a manageable way*). We could **reframe** his silence as an inability to speak, or even as a kind of paralysis born of fear of saying the wrong thing. Like Jamie in Chapter 3, John seems to want to avoid being noticed. But unlike Jamie, he doesn't suddenly erupt in any way, which means his difficulties could also go unnoticed.

Reframing feelings

We can use Framework 1 to **reframe** the teacher's feelings. The teacher is feeling helpless and unable to communicate both with John or about John. Rather than putting this feeling down to her own incompetence, this experience could be useful information for the teacher. It might be an example of where the unconscious defence mechanism of *projection* is operating (*see Chapter 3, p.57, for description of projection*): in other words, the teacher may be unconsciously picking up on a feeling that John is finding too hard to deal with. She also had an overwhelming feeling of sadness, but she can't say why she is feeling like this. Her sense of sadness and isolation may also be connected with how John is feeling. Often when we have feelings of sadness as a teacher, we try to 'get ourselves out of it', and to cheer up.

It might be worth taking time here to stop and think about the feeling. It could be valuable information about what is happening for the child.

The teacher here might also notice that she is trying to make herself feel better by asking John lots of questions, trying to get him to talk about how he feels. She is, however unintentionally, 'badgering' John, and causing him to withdraw further. So she could **reframe** her 'use*less*' feeling as providing her with use*ful* information on how John may be feeling. She could **reframe** her 'helping' questions as being intrusive, however unintentionally. Might this change of perspective cause her to adopt a different approach?

If you find yourself forgetting a child's name, you could **reframe** your understanding of why you do that as being somehow connected to a 'projection' from the child - as, for example, the consequence of the child's attempts to be invisible. There may be other instances - you forget or overlook this child altogether, for example, when choosing pupils to take on responsibilities in class, when making appointments for parents' evenings, when doing your seating plan - these children can sometimes quite literally disappear from our minds and our classes. Again, this is information for you. Why might they feel happier, or at least more comfortable, being overlooked? What is their experience of what happens when they were noticed in the past? Maybe not good things.

REFRAME • RESPOND

Strategies

✔ Notice your own feelings, and reframe your perspective on what you have been doing. Do you feel at a loss and sad about this child, and does this lead you to try even harder to interact with him? Maybe you spend more effort and energy on trying to create the very thing which this child finds hard - the relationship. Think more about working with this child through the task

✔ Notice if you are forgetting certain children. Make an effort to remember them - deliberately checking you have given them a job, sitting them closer to you, marking their name in the register with an asterix so that you consciously check you are remembering them as the day or lesson goes by.

STAGE 3   *REFLECT*

Reflect on the pupil's needs and feelings

Reviewing and **reframing** may lead us to wanting to take a different approach in working with a pupil who is quiet and withdrawn, and these may prove effective. However, with some pupils who behave like John, we will need to **reflect** further on their underlying needs if we really want to engage them in learning. We then have to consider those 3 key questions from Chapter 1:

> **What is the UNMET NEED the child is trying to fulfill through this behaviour?**
>
> **What has this child NOT had experience of?**
>
> **What is it that this child CANNOT believe about the teacher and the classroom?**

John's behaviour - not making eye-contact, withdrawing from any attempts at interaction - appears to show us that he needs space and a chance to retreat from people. Verbal interaction seems difficult. He takes refuge in his things and in clearly defined tasks which can be done in neat lines and boxes. This would suggest a need for safety, clear lines, boundaries, and an underlying anxiety about freer activities. Freer activities are those which develop more spontaneously, with fewer purely right and wrong answers. Speaking is a freer activity, where the outcome can't be easily predicted or controlled, and could be 'messy' if we don't know where it will lead. For some children, mess can feel dangerous. Let's look at why that might be.

FRAMEWORK 2 THE EFFECTS OF TRAUMA ON LEARNING

Although we might not know much about John's background and previous life experience, we can use the thinking from Framework 2 to get added insight into the possible reasons for John's behaviour. You might not have time or resources to find out exactly what's happened to him, but we can assume that his tendency to withdraw has served him well in other areas of his life, and has developed as a result of experience.

It might have been living with violence, and trying to make himself really small so as not to be noticed, to avoid drawing the violence his way. It could be the experience of living with a parent who had a mental illness, and not wanting to cause more trouble to a parent who was already finding it hard to cope with their own needs. There are many other possible reasons: not having an early experience of being talked to, not having had his feelings accepted and named, things not being discussed: his unrecognised little boy world may have shrunk to a carefully controlled, internal one. If this is what has happened, John will probably find it hard to believe that adults, such as teachers, will be able to notice him in a positive, caring way.

FRAMEWORK 3 ATTACHMENT PATTERN

In attachment terms, John, like Jamie (*in Chapter 3*), may be exhibiting an *insecure/avoidant* attachment pattern. He feels safe in the tasks but not in the relationship with the teacher within the Learning Triangle. We insist on trying to have a relationship, as we know it's important for learning. Our insistence and his reluctance result in the child withdrawing further from the relationship, the exact opposite effect of what we are hoping to achieve. Ultimately, John needs to learn how to use the relationship, but again, this will be through the third point in the triangle, maybe the task, maybe another pupil, or by being given a responsibility within the class, such as the job of giving out the books at the start of the lesson.

FRAMEWORK 4 PLAY DEVELOPMENT

In play terms, John doesn't appear to be able to play *with*, but he may be able to play *alongside*. In developmental terms he may have missed out on the 'with' stage of play development, perhaps because he hasn't been in an environment where he could invite other children in to play and negotiate the rules of their games together. If John spent his early years trying to make sure he didn't draw potentially dangerous adult attention to himself, he may never have had the opportunity to play with other children in a noisy, interactive way.

Bearing all this in mind, we can develop another set of strategies based on meeting John's current needs, planning to develop those skills he doesn't yet have. Essentially, he needs to practise skills which gradually bring him out into the external world, and which gently help him relate to and notice others in a safe way.

REFLECT • RESPOND

Strategies

I   LESSON PLANNING

✔ Plan tasks which encourage John to work with others but give him a clear role, for example, a jigsaw reading, where he has some of the answers and has to share them with the group in order to complete the activity. Similarly, activities in which John and a partner have to exchange information to complete a task can develop the skill of interacting

✔ Create tasks where the whole group or smaller groups have to work collaboratively to put something together. For example, everyone has a different word and the group has to arrange them to form a sentence or set of instructions

✔ Re-group pairwork in different ways. For example, some students have a picture, and others have a description of it. They have to find their partner, and then work together on a task. This structured task will encourage children such as John to interact on a small scale with another pupil. The important part of the task, which keeps it safe for the child who finds unpredictable contact with others threatening, is that each child has a *clear* role

✔ Use tasks which allow the pupil's part to be 'boxed'. Create worksheets where pupils have to draw or put their answers in sections which have frames around them. For some children, simply putting a frame around a piece of work, writing or drawing, can help him or her feel contained. Similarly, use worksheets which involve putting things into shapes, columns, or colour-coded groups, as these may help assuage his anxiety about the need for order

✔ Notice what the child is good at or interested in. If possible, bring some of this into your lesson plan. For example, if John is interested in cars and you want the class to work on a collage, bring in some car magazines. However, how you present them will be crucial. Avoid saying *"I brought these in because I thought you might like them"*. This is too direct and relationship-based. Instead, say something more like: *"There are lots of cars here and I am not sure which one is the best"*. This invites the pupil to discuss the content of the topic and engage in the relationship through the task

✔ This child will find it very difficult to talk about feelings. Talking about feeling involves trusting a relationship, taking a risk and not knowing the end result. Children like John often respond to characters in stories, video, newspapers, history and coursebooks. Build these tasks into your planning and work through the characters to develop a relationship around them.

For example, if you are studying a certain period in history, create a task such as a journal written by a boy from that time which will allow John to express feelings through the character.

When you comment on the work, comment on the possible feelings and experiences of the character, rather than your own impression of what he's written:

"That boy seems to find it really hard to survive in that big, violent community. I wonder how he feels" rather than *"I really like the way you have described that boy".*

The first comment keeps the reference to feelings safe within the metaphor

✔ Plan to give the pupil jobs which involve some interaction with others, for example, handing out books at the start of a lesson. Be careful, however, that your job does not isolate them further from your class. For example, children such as John often seem to be chosen to take messages around to other classes, in effect, removing them completely for a period of time from their class!

II   PLANNING DEVELOPMENTAL TASKS

✔ If you have the chance to include some warm-up or brain-break activities in your class, choose games which encourage these children to look outward, but in a fun way. For example, you might use circle time to play some quick 'noticing' games such as 'Use your eyes'.

◉ **ACTIVITY Use your eyes   (warm-up/ice-breaker)**

Students can work in pairs or 3s. Begin by asking them to shut their eyes and try to remember the colour of their partner's eyes. Then, ask them to take a moment and look at each other to form a picture in their minds.

One person from each pair or group then goes out of the room. They change three things about their appearance and come back into the room. Their partner must look and find the three changes.

III   PLANNING FOR OUTSIDE CLASS TIME

✔ Find out what the child is good at or interested in. Make use of any clubs or after school activities which promote this. You may need to enlist the help of another child to encourage John to go to the first few meetings of such a club

✔ If you have the opportunity for someone to work individually with the child, make use of stories such as *Willy and the Wobbly House* (Sunderland, 2001), which explore how to deal with anxieties about keeping things under control, orderly and in straight lines. These stories may appear to be aimed at younger children as they are designed as colourful picture books. However, they can be successfully used with older pupils who may be operating at a much younger emotional age than their chronological age. When presenting these stories to older pupils, it may be necessary to find a way to make them seem appropriate.

You can say, "*I think these stories are great and I'd like you to help me decide who they might be helpful for*".

Alternatively, you can address the issue directly and say, "*I know these books look like they are written for younger children but I think they are really great and useful for all ages. Let's see what you think".* In my experience, once they are given a legitimate reason for dipping into the book, the pupils get hooked by the stories

✔ Small groups which work on creative, artistic projects, such as making cards for celebrations, collages or mosaics, can be very helpful as they allow the child to get messy, have fun and learn not to worry about keeping everything absolutely neat. It will be important, however, for this child to be involved in putting things out at the beginning and the putting away, tidying up and sorting at the end of such an activity, as otherwise it will all feel too uncontained for them.

You'll know a kid who has been withdrawn is making progress when …

★ *you can remember his name without much prompting*

★ *he can put his bag away at the start of the lesson and not spend the lesson searching around in it*

★ *he can work on a project with at least one other pupil*

★ *he can take part in an activity which involves a bit of mess and even disorganisation, for example, a school sports day*

★ *he is seen having a laugh with another pupil …*

and sometimes,

★ *you have to reprimand him for talking and not getting on with his work!*

Chapter 5

"What can I do with the kid who… bullies the teacher?"

Peter is fourteen and causing concern to many staff. His Head of Year says:

> *"Peter is a bully. He bullies other children but he also attempts to bully and intimidate staff. I've told staff that I will attend meetings with them if they don't want to be alone with him. Female staff say that he's very offensive and uses sexual language. He is a nasty piece of work, and very threatening"*

Another teacher says:

> *"He loves getting to me and winding me up. I am sure he enjoys thinking of new ways to do that"*

Peter says:

> *"The teachers here hate me. They think I'm aggressive, but I'm not. I'm just big and I have a loud voice. They're not interested in listening to me. They're out to get me, none of them like me, they just want me out".*

Using the RETHINK model to think about Peter

We can see from the comments above that Peter's behaviour is considered very challenging by staff. Peter and his teachers seem to feel very negative towards each other, and this is obviously impeding teaching and learning. We can use the **RETHINK** model to think about what is happening in the interaction between Peter and staff. Any insight we gain will help us to develop support and strategies for this seemingly impossible situation.

STAGE I *REVIEW*

Review what is happening in class at the moment

This is a very emotive and difficult experience for all concerned. Staff are feeling personally attacked by Peter. Peter is feeling persecuted by teachers. We need to find an objective way of understanding what's going on. That isn't to say that we can dismiss the emotions, but that we need to find a starting point which allows us to really stand back and clearly observe what is actually happening.

We can begin by **reviewing** the language used about Peter. We can tell from the words used by both staff and Peter that emotions are running extremely high. Negative and harsh judgments are being made on all sides. If we look closely at the actual choice of words being used, we can see that there are several statements which comment on Peter's identity, statements which begin with *"He is…"*: for example, *"He is a nasty piece of work"*, *"He is a bully"*. Moreover, there are only assumptions of negative intentions behind the behaviour: *"He loves winding me up"*. Although staff might *feel* this is true, it doesn't explain what Peter is actually doing. Staff are apparently in total agreement about the negative impact of Peter's behaviour. This isn't unusual; when a child seems to be intimidating staff, our natural reaction is to support and defend our colleagues. Also, Peter is a large boy, and his body language and presence can seem physically threatening. Instinctively, we tend to respond differently to someone larger and more physically powerful than us, and it can be difficult to recognise that this may be influencing how we interpret their behaviour.

So at first glance, there appears to be little common ground between staff and the pupil. Interestingly, there's no indication of what Peter is like at learning. No-one has commented on his work or his ability to do a task. We can assume that his behaviour and the feelings it evokes are getting in the way of relationships and learning.

In our **review** of what's actually happening, we now need to go back to basics and look at how the situation is currently being managed. Is there a behaviour plan in place for dealing with Peter? Do all the staff know about it? Has Peter been involved in drawing it up? Are there rewards for appropriate behaviour as well as sanctions for inappropriate behaviour? Is there a clear back-up plan for removing Peter from the class if necessary, and how is this achieved? Do staff support each other with concrete offers of help and support with the withdrawal?

What happens in class when Peter is behaving appropriately? Is this acknowledged and noticed? A child such as Peter is often overlooked when he isn't bullying and shouting, as staff are just relieved that he is sitting quietly. We can **review** the timing, triggers (*see p.7*) and length of Peter's outbursts. How often do they happen, and when? For example, if the behaviour kicks in at the end of lesson before a break, what is it about the break that makes this child want to act out so that he might be kept back? Do the outbursts always happen at the beginning of a class? In which case, how do we greet Peter? Is it with a smile and a positive comment (very difficult if we're feeling very negative towards him) or is it with a frown, silence, or comment such as *"Let's hope you can behave better than last time"*. This type of comment may well trigger a memory of the previous negative interaction, and will more than likely set up a new one. It's very important for staff to work on managing their own state (*see strategies, below*) before teaching a pupil like Peter.

Does Peter have any unmet learning needs? This kind of behaviour often masks poor literacy or low self-confidence when faced with written tasks. It may seem better to Peter and other boys like him to be in trouble because of abusive behaviour, rather than to be 'shown up' in terms of learning needs.

We can also **review** the whole-school situation for the 'Peter' in our classroom. How is he talked about in the staffroom? It may well be that the teachers who are having problems speak the most about him, and that those who aren't experiencing difficulties with him don't want to sound as if they are being disloyal or competitive by saying, *"He's alright with me"*. It might be worth asking if there's anyone he *does* work well for, and if there is, looking at the key differences between this and every other situation. In this **review**, we can also look at what Peter is good at or seems interested in - maybe music or sport? Who else do we know who can work with him on this? Or who might be willing to try?

REVIEW • RESPOND

Strategies

- ✔ Be clear and consistent about your classroom management and procedures, and make sure that you're following them
- ✔ Have a clearly agreed plan in place to deal with Peter, with clear targets which have been agreed separately with the pupil
- ✔ If you notice Peter's behaviour is triggered at certain times in the lesson or during the day, plan appropriate support for him at those times
- ✔ Deal with any unmet learning needs: for example, arrange extra literacy support
- ✔ Choose to record times which are non-conflictual, and notice what's happening at those times
- ✔ Try to find things which Peter is good at and work with these. For example, you might notice that he's very good at drawing and talk to the art teacher about him doing some posters for your class
- ✔ Find ways to manage your own emotional state when dealing with pupils

such as Peter. For example, you might choose to talk to a supportive colleague before the lesson, in order to remind yourself of your strengths and strategies. You might use this time to think together about how best to deal with your emotions and actions in relation to Peter. Sitting in the staffroom before your lesson and venting your anger with colleagues who all agree with you about Peter might seem cathartic, but it can be counter-productive and lead you to feel worse. It is very difficult to deal with our feelings about bullying alone, so we do need to talk it through with a colleague who can listen without becoming condemnatory of either Peter or yourself

(For more ideas on managing your own state, see Appendix B)

✔ Practise taking a deep breath when conflict seems to be starting: take a literal step back and give yourself time to think, rather than being drawn into retaliating as a peer might (as opposed to a thinking adult)

✔ Decide what you are going to say in the first few minutes to greet Peter, so that you get off to a positive start. Keep the focus wherever possible on learning and draw his attention to this as well.

For example, you can say *"OK Peter, I know you have good ideas, so let's get started and you can help us with this brainstorm"*, rather than *"We are waiting for you to sit down and stop distracting everyone"*. The second sentence gives power to Peter's behaviour, and does not draw his attention to learning at all

By **reviewing** the behaviour management plan for Peter and looking at what's working well, we may find that Peter's behaviour becomes less challenging to deal with. Some pupils respond to a strong, consistently applied plan. However, for some pupils, this won't be enough. Their behaviour is driven by other factors, which we'll need to consider.

STAGE 2 *REFRAME*

We might need help in changing the way we think and talk about Peter. Staff are often told to *'find something to like'* about pupils who behave as Peter does, but it can seem impossible when we're feeling bullied and intimidated. We can use the **reframe** stage of the **RETHINK** model to separate a description of Peter's behaviour from our judgment or interpretation of it. If we're able to do this, we can focus on the really clear and precise details of what Peter is actually doing that is causing problems, and **reframe** our responses.

When asked, *"What is Peter doing specifically that you interpret as intimidating?"* a classroom teacher describes it as follows:

BEHAVIOUR	INTERPRETATIONS AND FEELINGS
"When I'm presenting, Peter often stands up and walks over to another pupil	*… I **feel** as if I am a nobody to him*
When I tell him to sit down, he usually says he needs a rubber and laughs	*… I **feel** really uneasy and intimidated*
If I insist he sits down, he usually walks back slowly, saying something loudly, like "What's her problem? Mustn't have got any last night"	*… I **feel** unsure what to do and actually want to cry"*

We can see that if we try to describe Peter's behaviour without our own feelings and interpretations, we can at least become clearer on what the issues are. In difficult situations such as the one described above, our ability to take action can be impeded by our own hard-to-manage feelings. We really need to take a step back, and focus on what to do in response to the actual behaviour. Moreover, we need to talk to Peter about his behaviour in a specific and objective way, so that he can't side-track the issue. Actually describing the behaviour in specific detail, whilst not making light of its impact, will make it seem more manageable and something which we can hope to influence. We also need to notice that by continuing to use words such as 'disruptive' and 'aggressive' when talking to the pupil, we can find ourselves in no-win situations, where the conversation goes something like this:

> *"You were very disruptive and aggressive in my class"*
> *"No, I wasn't!" "Yes, you were!" "No, I wasn't"*

All these elements indicate that we now need to think about how to respond to Peter walking around the classroom when he should be sitting down. We also need to think about what we're going to do when he uses inappropriate language, particularly in response to being corrected. Finally, we need to know what we're going to do or say when the situation seems to be escalating, and we decide that Peter needs to leave the class. In classroom management terms, we can see there are two main issues - what to do *in the moment,* in response to Peter's behaviour, and how to take *further action* if we can't cope with what's happening in the classroom. With this type of pupil, it may indeed be necessary to effect a removal from the class, but even this can be done in a constructive way which allows the pupil to save face, and the teacher to talk to him at another time to repair the relationship.

REFRAME • RESPOND
Strategies
MORE CLASSROOM MANAGEMENT
By focusing very specifically on what is happening and your interpretation of it, you can develop an extra set of classroom management strategies.

✔ Notice when you are making negative identity level statements about a pupil. Choose to focus on precisely what's happening, and how it's making you feel. For example, *"He is a nasty piece of work"* is more concrete and harder to work with than *"When he shouts at me and uses offensive language, I find it very hard to find anything to like about him"*. The second re-phrasing gives you a chance to think: *"OK, and at other times, maybe there are things I can find to like about him"*. You can then address the behaviour specifically, and not your interpretation of it

✔ Use identity level statements positively, to create an aspiration for the pupil to live up to. Strive to see the positive intention or higher aspiration, for example: *"You are usually a person with good manners, there is no need for you to talk like that"*

✔ Remember that not everything needs to be dealt with immediately and in the moment. Have a clear back-up plan for removing the pupil from your class, knowing how you'll do it and who he'll go to. For example, say *"You are not in a good state for learning today; you need to leave and go to Mr/s X as we agreed, and we will talk about this later"*

✔ Avoid being drawn into negotiation and discussion at this point. You will probably have to wait longer than is comfortable for you, but stand firm. You can take a later opportunity to talk to the student about his needs and how to repair the situation

✔ Avoid being drawn into reactions to the secondary behaviour. By secondary behaviour, I mean things the pupil will do or say that are distracting and not related to the main issue. For example, when asked to sit down, Peter might sigh loudly, roll his eyes, and start wandering slowly over to his desk. None of these behaviours are your primary focus; you just want Peter to go back to his desk and he is doing that, albeit with a great show of reluctance. If you get drawn into commenting about the sighing, eye rolling or telling him to hurry up, you offer him the stage. Be clear what needs to happen in that moment:

"I need you to sit down so that we can get on with learning"

✔ Your use of language will be vital. Make conscious decisions to use language which does not escalate conflict. For example: use 'we' where possible, and refer to any previous agreement: *"We agreed that you would sit here"*

✔ Match the pupil's voice, tone, body language and key words of the pupils. For example, if the pupil is standing up, stand up as well, and speak in a strong voice but not at the same volume

✔ Say what *you want* to happen, not what you don't want. For example: *"Sit down and focus on your work,"* rather than *"Stop walking around and interfering with other people's work"*. The first comment encourages the brain to focus on the required action, and does not imply any blame related to what Peter is doing with other people

✔ Use short sentences and logical sequencing so that the brain can be clear what is wanted. For example, *"Open your books and look at the board"* rather than *"Before looking at the board, I want you to open your books"*. The brain hears and responds to the action words in the order they appear

✔ Start difficult conversations by 'stacking up' things which you know the other person will have to agree with: *"I've asked you to stay behind and you are not very happy about that: you want to get out of here as soon as possible, and we both need to get this sorted"* (stacking up means saying a list of things which the pupil's brain will automatically agree with). This means that when you do start discussing the issue, the pupil will have already come some way internally towards meeting you

✔ Don't make idle threats. The kind of behaviour Peter is demonstrating often provokes us into a desire to retaliate and punish, but we need to remember that we are the adults, and we need to show the pupil that everyone is treated fairly and consistently. A pupil who has been humiliated by an over-severe punishment will harbour resentment and find other ways to spoil things for themselves, the teacher and the class.

✔ Practise calming and distancing yourself from your own extreme emotions in the moment. For example, you could choose a memorable word, phrase or song lyric you can say to yourself to manage your feelings (see *creating positive anchors, Appendix B*)

✔ Use the 'broken record' technique. Decide what you are going to say and keep it simple. Repeat it calmly. Re-wording and justifying will draw you into unnecessary, protracted, off-task discussions

REFRAMING THE FEELINGS

As described above, **reframe** by separating out the behaviour and your interpretation of it. Acknowledge the feelings the behaviour evokes in you and manage your own state. It might help to say to yourself, *"This is not meant for me personally"*, and *"He is seeking a certain reaction: I will not do what is expected".*

✔ Give power in other ways rather than being drawn into a continual battle for supremacy in front of the whole class. For example, once Peter has sat down, you do not need to continue to prove that you have power over him. At that point, you could give him a choice about how to start the next activity. *"OK, good, you now need to do this worksheet, you can write on the sheet or in your book"*

✔ Reframe the pupil's behaviour by asking yourself how you would interpret it if you were dealing with a younger, smaller child. Pupils such as Peter are often operating at a younger emotional age than their chronological age. They may be big, tall and loud, but in many ways they react emotionally like a toddler who has not learned to manage their own overwhelming feelings

✔ Reframe the behaviour with a positive intention. You can choose to do this just for your own thinking or you can choose to name it to the student. Examples of this kind of reframe might be: *"There are other ways of getting noticed. You can be funny without insulting people"*

"I wonder what you expect from me here"

"You don't need to be like that **here***"*

"Usually when someone does (the behaviour), they are not getting heard in some other way: maybe you want me/us to notice you… perhaps we need to find other ways for you to get noticed appropriately"

STAGE 3 *REFLECT*

Reflect on the pupil's needs and feelings

With some children, the strategies outlined above may be enough for us to be able to manage their challenging behaviour. However, for pupils like Peter, there are often deep, underlying needs which have not been met in their early years and which are now driving their behaviour in class. It can be hard to think about the needs of a boy like Peter. When our own emotions and personal feelings are hurt, the child's needs can get lost. Our challenge is to take a step back from our own hurt and try to deal as objectively as possible with the behaviour, so that we can then re-focus on the learning. We can use the 3 key questions from Chapter 1 to help us to do this:

> **What is the UNMET NEED the child is trying to fulfill through this behaviour?**
>
> **What has this child NOT had experience of?**
>
> **What is it that this child CANNOT believe about the teacher and the classroom?**

FRAMEWORK I WHERE THE FEELINGS COME FROM

We can see that Peter seems unable to recognise his feelings or name them. He expresses all his pent-up feelings through insults and attacks on the teacher. He also appears to be unable to let the adult have a good opinion of him. He is spoiling, and doesn't allow teaching to take place. The teacher feels humiliated, threatened, and not valued. This may be a clear projection of how Peter is feeling most of the time in his dealings with adults, perhaps as a result of his earliest experience of relationships (*for more on projection see p.57*).

By being offensive, rude and bullying towards staff, Peter is not giving staff any chance of offering him their kindness and support. It is likely that they are being drawn into enacting the part of the punitive adults from his past, caught up in the transference and counter-transference (*for more on transference and counter-transference, see below*).

We should note that there is a difference between bullying peers and bullying staff: students who bully staff, but do not 'take on' their peers, are often quite fearful. Their need is to exert power over others in school to keep their anxiety at bay about being powerless in situations outside school. So their need might not be 'just' to exert power for its own sake, but to keep themselves safe from their uncontained feelings of anxiety and terror.

FRAMEWORK 2 THE EFFECTS OF TRAUMA ON LEARNING

It appears that Peter needs to let us know that he cannot trust or allow any gentleness. This would suggest that he has not experienced tenderness of this kind in his early years: in fact, he may have experienced just the opposite, and has learnt to expect anger and humiliation in his dealings with adults. It is possible that he has lived in a traumatising, violent environment,where kind, gentle feelings are not valued, feelings of pain are ignored or suppressed, and he is regularly humiliated (*see* Batmanghelidj, in Perry, 2009, p.175). As a result, he can't believe that the teacher will not use his or her position to bully and abuse if given the chance. This has affected his ability to make use of relationships with teachers for learning. His need to keep himself safe means he is unable to seek or accept help from the staff; he can't bear not knowing something as this reminds him of humiliation, and he is unable to manage the frustration, anxiety and disappointment inherent in learning something new.

We can therefore list Peter's needs as
* the need to feel safe in the school, safe from possible humiliation and abuse of power
* the need to trust that the adults and the school building itself can provide boundaries and a containing structure, and that the teachers can cope with and manage his overwhelming, unbearable feelings
* the need to have his feelings recognised, named and, wherever possible, reflected back in a manageable way
* the need to have adults help him find ways to settle his anxiety at the start of lessons or at 'trigger' points, so that he can believe he can learn
* the need to learn that the teacher-pupil relationship can be a shared dialogue, rather than a battle over who holds the power
* the need to experience learning as an empowering, fun activity, rather than a potentially humiliating experience

Teachers often find themselves reacting to a pupil who behaves like Peter in a sarcastic, punitive or defensive way. They can find themselves thinking, *"I'm not afraid of him. I can take him on"*. This kind of pattern may be an example of *transference,* where the adult and the child are unconsciously recreating a relationship from the past.

Transference and counter-transference
Transference may be at work, when, for example, feelings and attitudes from a

relationship with a child's main carers from the past are 'transferred' and are played out, or re-experienced, in a later relationship with a teacher. An adult who begins to make a significant relationship with the child can then get caught up in the pattern the child is unconsciously creating around them. If you have similar feelings toward the 'Peter' in your class as the teacher described on p.84, it might be useful to ask yourself if you are being caught up in a counter-transference situation. This might well be the case if you find yourself reacting in what is for you an untypical way, somehow fulfilling the child's learned expectations.

We can work with this 'transference' from other relationships by giving the child an experience of a different way of relating. If we begin to notice the pattern of interaction, we may be able to stop ourselves being 'pulled in' and do something different to break the negative pattern. This is what Peter needs from the adults around him.

Be aware that the type of behaviour 'Peter' presents in your classroom will hook you into any of your own issues about bullying, abuse of power, victimisation, and your own gut reactions to feeling threatened. It can often drag you back into your own adolescence. You can find yourself in a transference/counter-transference situation, where Peter's behaviour triggers a re-enactment of one of your own earlier relationships. This mutual triggering of reminders from the past can create a downward spiral for both you and the child, where you do not have a relationship with each other but rather a relationship based on memories of other negative interactions. It is essential that you, as the adult, notice this and take responsibility for changing it. For example, Catherine, a teacher in a secondary school described how the downward spiral worked for her.

"I was working with a group of teenage girls on a project about self-esteem and bullying. They continually seemed to pick on me, commenting on my hair, my clothes, my accent, everything really. I found myself getting upset and distancing myself from them, letting them go on the computer rather than do discussion activities as I usually do. I realised that I had been

taken right back in my own mind to being a 14 year old girl who did not fit in. Being in this group brought it all back to me, and I realised I was behaving in the way I did when I was 14 - excluding myself from the group when in fact, as the adult, I needed to lead the group!".

If you find this happening, you, as the adult, need to think: *"Break the pattern. Just do something different, anything!"*

Above all, remember that you do not have to have all the answers. You can be a 'good-enough' teacher, and you do not need to be perfect. Ask for and offer help to colleagues who are experiencing this kind of challenge. If you are having problems with this pupil, it is highly likely that others are as well. When we feel helpless and bullied, it is often very difficult to speak to others about it. We assume there is something wrong with us and that everyone else could deal with the situation effectively. If you find yourself thinking like this, you are thinking like a victim of bullying. Think about the advice you would give a child who is being bullied: you would advise them to talk about it to a trusted adult - take your own advice! We know that discussing situations with colleagues can help us develop a shared response, and this is vital in this instance.

FRAMEWORK 3 ATTACHMENT PATTERN

In attachment terms, Peter may be showing a profile of *insecure/disorganised* attachment behaviour. He is not 'doing' the task or the relationship. He needs some kind of contained, safe structure with adults who can support each other, before he can focus on the task or the relationship. This will involve key staff in the school preparing a plan, ensuring especially there is a plan for 'blow-up' times (particularly significant if there is going to be a change in routine or teacher): preferably with a key attachment figure to work individually with Peter as well. These staff would also need to have regular meetings around the child, not called as *re*active but as *pro*active meetings.

FRAMEWORK 4 PLAY DEVELOPMENT

In play terms, Peter cannot play by other people's rules. His behaviour with his peers would suggest he can socialise, but only on his own terms. He wants to control the game and set the rules. Playing by rules which are set by others may feel like giving them the chance to exercise power over him, something which he cannot allow for fear of humiliation.

REFLECT • RESPOND

Strategies

I   PLANNING

✔ Be proactive and set up a staff support group to look at anything that works with Peter. This might not always be examples from a classroom situation, but ask: what is going on in these constructive situations, and what are people doing that helps? When Peter's Head of Year thought about this, he realised that Peter had a good relationship with the school caretaker, whom he often chatted to. The caretaker said:

"I like Peter, he is just a normal lad, I was a bit like that myself. I think he just doesn't like being cooped up in a classroom. We usually talk about my work and the aviary I have at home".

Peter as 'a
normal lad' and can empathise with Peter not liking classrooms

✔ School offers Peter a structure and routine. Ensure as far as possible that this routine is consistent. If there are going to be changes, try to flag these up in advance or acknowledge the potential difficulty for him

✔ Take a step back from your feelings about the insults and think what they are telling you about the child's needs. Insults can be indicative of how the pupil is feeling about himself. Children who regularly call others 'stupid', often feel stupid themselves

II   ON THE SPOT RESPONSES

✔ Keep your language and responses simple and clear. Choose a phrase
and stick to it. This child needs a strong containing adult who can think,
and comments expressed in consistent language.

For example: *"You don't need to be like that* **here***"*

"You can manage yourself. You know what to do"

"You know the right behaviour and you are able to do it"

✔ If you choose to see the child's behaviour as telling you about a need,
what will you do? You might say:

*"Sometimes people say bad things about other people because they are feeling
bad themselves"*

*"You're acting very angry now. I wonder who or what exactly you are angry
with?"*

Such comments won't automatically cause changes in the pupil's
behaviour. In fact, you might get a negative reaction in the moment, with
the pupil rejecting your comment and saying something like *"Don't be
stupid, what a load of rubbish"* (or worse); but he will have heard it, and it
will filter into his thinking. Children who haven't had an experience of
their feelings being understood and named will find the acknowledgement
of emotions very hard to bear. However, by trying to understand and
reflect back to them, you will be beginning a process of gradual change.

✔ For some reason this pupil cannot allow gentleness. You could choose to
address his need to allow kind behaviour by showing Peter you are not
treating him aggressively

*"I don't speak to you like that. I don't like it when you speak to me like that.
There is no need to speak like that"*

*"You know that isn't appropriate. I know that you have better manners than
that. I wonder why you do it?"*

III   PLANNING OUTSIDE CLASS

✔ A child like Peter will need a significant adult to help him develop the skills needed to access learning. If you can provide this kind of time, the adult can get to know Peter and what he is good at

✔ It can also be useful to use therapeutic stories such as *A Wibble Called Bipley* and *How Hattie Hated Kindness* (Sunderland, 2001) to help Peter learn to name and understand 'bad' feelings (*see p.77 on the use of such stories*)

✔ Shared storywriting can work well, where the adult starts the story and then the child continues. They then take turns to write, with the adult trying to comment on any themes or issues which are arising for the characters in the story, being careful to stay in the metaphor

You'll know a kid who bullies the teacher is making progress when ...

★ *he is sent out of class fewer times (there will probably still be incidents, but there should be less of them, or less serious ones)*

★ *he can get down to some work without the whole lesson being taken up with dealing with his behaviour*

★ *he reduces the frequency of his negative comments about other kids and staff*

★ *other pupils don't mind working with him*

★ *you can think of positive things to say about him or know things he is good at*

★ *he can show some empathy with other children or staff*

★ *he is not continually discussed in the staffroom!*

Chapter 6

"What can I do with the kid who… can't sit still?"

Megan is eight and doesn't appear to be able to sit stll in her class.
Her teacher says,

> "Teaching Megan gives me a headache. She's always wandering around
> the class, picking up pens and other stuff from other children's tables. She
> never pays attention and she's always distracting others in the class with
> her behaviour. She's like a spinning top which has been wound up and just
> can't stop. Her Teaching Assistant is practically glued to her side, but it
> means she's continually up and down as well, getting Megan to sit down,
> focus, do her work, and that's just as distracting. She is not particularly
> confrontational or anything, but I'm sure the other pupils in the class find
> her behaviour just as irritating as I do".

Using the RETHINK model for thinking about Megan

Megan is an example of a pupil who does not directly challenge the teacher's authority
but whose constant moving around the class, picking things up and getting distracted
from her work interrupts both the teaching and learning. We can use the **RETHINK**
model to get some insight into what is happening for Megan in the classroom.

STAGE 1 *REVIEW*

Review what is happening in class at the moment

We can begin by **reviewing** and closely observing what is happening with Megan at the moment in class. With this type of pupil, it is vital to **review** our classroom management strategies to ensure consistency and clarity of boundaries.

Are the classroom rules clear? Have they been set with the pupils and are they re-visited regularly? What happens when Megan keeps getting up and moving around the class? Does she get a lot of attention from the teaching staff? It's very likely that she does, even if it's negative attention in the form of reprimands for her behaviour. What happens when she is engaged and on-task? Does this get noticed? Or does Megan's appropriate behaviour get overlooked, because she isn't bringing herself to our attention? We can also **review** the level of work and type of task.   Is Megan actually able to do the work? How do we know? What kind of tasks engages her and keeps her in her seat? Is her behaviour affected by time of day and type of lesson? Does she behave like this when particular children are nearby, or is what she does affected by certain topics?

CHARACTERISTICS OF A PUPIL WITH ADHD

In terms of **inattention**, a student would present with **at least six** of the following **for at least six months**, to a degree that is maladaptive and inconsistent with his or her developmental level:

(a) often fails to give close attention to details or makes careless mistakes in schoolwork or other activities

(b) often has difficulty sustaining attention in tasks or play activities

(c) often doesn't seem to listen when spoken to directly

(d) often doesn't follow through on instructions and fails to finish school work

(e) often has difficulty organising tasks and activities

(f) often avoids, dislikes, or is reluctant to engage in tasks that require sustained mental effort

(g) often loses things necessary for tasks or activities (for example, toys, school assignments, pencils, books)

(h) is often easily distracted by extraneous stimuli

(i) is often forgetful in daily activities

Are we catering for Megan's learning style in our lesson planning? She might be a kinaesthetic learner who needs to move around and touch things. When we look at practical lessons such as painting and PE, we can observe whether her behaviour is a problem in these subjects as well.

If Megan is behaving in the same way across all classes, it might be necessary to arrange an assessment for her with an Educational Psychologist, for a possible diagnosis of ADHD (*see below*). It's possible, of course, that Megan's behaviour could also be understood in terms of an early disrupted attachment experience (*see p.105*), at the same time as she is exhibiting traits of ADHD. In either case, it can be useful to get an assessment in order to focus on what she needs from the teacher and the classroom.

It's important to get a child's needs assessed if there is a problem across the school. But we can get distracted by labels and diagnoses. Whether a child has a diagnosis of ADHD or not is to some extent irrelevant when you're faced with the actual behaviour in the classroom. Even if the 'Megan' in your class has this diagnosis, you'll need to work on ensuring your classroom management strategies are clear, consistent and regularly enforced. The following strategies will benefit all pupils, regardless of whether or not they've been assessed with an extra learning difficulty.

In terms of **hyperactivity/ impulsivity**, a student would present with **at least six** of the following **for at least six months**, to a degree that is maladaptive and inconsistent with developmental level:

Factors relating to hyperactivity

(a) often fidgets with hands or feet or squirms in seat

(b) often leaves seat in classroom or in other situations in which remaining seated is expected

(c) often runs about or climbs excessively in inappropriate situations

(d) often has difficulty playing or engaging in leisure activities quietly

(e) is often 'on the go' or acts as if 'driven by a motor'

(f) often talks excessively

Factors relating to impulsivity

(g) often blurts out answers before questions have been completed

(h) often has difficulty awaiting turn

(i) often interrupts or intrudes on others (for example, butts into conversations)

REVIEW • RESPOND

Strategies

I   LESSON PLANNING

✔ Use short, timed activities and short-term goals

✔ Reduce the amount of materials available during activities by having the student put away unnecessary items. Have a special place for tools, materials, and books

✔ Notice and use any strengths the pupil has. For example, if Megan is good at organising, give her the task of keeping the classroom resources such as pens, rulers and paper tidy and organised at the beginning and end of every lesson

✔ Make use of computer-assisted learning: it can help this kind of child to 'tune out' other distractions and work at their own pace

II   CLASSROOM MANAGEMENT

✔ Seating plan. Seat these children in the front near the teacher with their backs to the rest of the class: surround them with significant good peer models and encourage co-operative learning. Avoid all distracting stimuli. Try not to place pupils near air conditioners, high traffic areas, heaters, doors, windows, or anything else that could be equally stimulating or agitating

✔ Rules and routines. Make few rules and frame them in the positive, but enforce them

✔ Develop routines and techniques for starting and stopping work and for getting silence.
For example: *"OK, let's see the first ten students to face me"*
"I will clap 3 times and everyone needs to be facing me by the last clap"
"When you see me put my hand up, put your own hand up and stop talking"
"When I turn off the lights, you need to stop the activity and look at me"

✔ When you ask a question, say the pupil's name first and then pause for a few seconds as a signal for him/her to pay attention

III   GIVING INSTRUCTIONS

✔ Maintain eye contact during verbal instructions

✔ Provide models of what's expected. Give an example of what pupils need to do and get an example from them to check they understand

✔ Simplify complex directions. Avoid multiple commands. Give action words first, avoid sequencers. So, instead of: *"Before opening your books, look at the board"*, say … *"Look at the board. Open your books."*

✔ Assign only one task at a time

✔ Match what you are doing to what you are saying.

Are you unwittingly adding to the chaos in Megan's mind?

For example, when you want to give an instruction to students to stop what they are doing, stand still.

If you're roaming around the room and asking pupils to stop, you are giving a mixed message. Children like Megan will get confused.

STAGE 2 *REFRAME*

The 'Megan' in your class may present with many of the symptoms listed on p.98 for a diagnosis of ADHD. You could, however, also **reframe** her 'symptoms' as perfectly normal responses to a turbulent environment. Children who have lived in violent, chaotic environments may have learned to be hyper-vigilant and anxious all the time. They've no idea where the next threat may come from, so they can't focus for too long on one thing: becoming absorbed can feel risky to them. Their anxiety levels are very high, and this can present in class as agitated, fidgety behaviour, with an inability to focus on a task.

Teachers often say the child isn't paying attention. It might be helpful to **reframe** this thought. It is not that Megan is NOT paying attention, but it's that she *is* paying attention, but to too many things at once, and can't prioritise what to pay attention to. She is paying attention to something, but just not to what the teacher wants!

So fidgeting and the inability to sit still can be **reframed** as anxiety about the classroom situation, and not knowing where the next threat might come from. Another **reframing** for the kid who can't sit still is that her brain may be too full up with other things to have space to concentrate on schoolwork. We need to take both these factors into consideration when we're trying to understand the child better, and when planning our teaching strategies.

REFRAME • RESPOND

Strategies

✔ Even if the child has been diagnosed with ADHD, all of the above might be true. These children often feel very abnormal and different. You can help by reframing the way their brain works as something normal and controllable.

For example, I often ask children what percentage of their brain they feel they are in control of. Generally, they say something like 50%, and we can then say:

"This is what we can work with and what you can manage".

This affirming message lets them know that they still have the power to change their behaviour: it is not something completely unmanageable

✔ We can also name the anxiety they may be holding in their minds, either consciously or unconsciously:

"Maybe your brain is so full up of other stuff that you are finding it hard to concentrate today".

Again, this lets them know that there are good reasons for their inability to concentrate, and suggests that there's something which can be done to improve the situation

(for example, making a different space and time to pay some attention to 'the other stuff')

STAGE 3 *REFLECT*

Reflect on the pupil's needs and feelings

With some pupils, the strategies and thinking outlined above may be enough to help the teacher and the child to manage their behaviour better in class. However, if the behaviour persists, it may be showing us that the child has other unmet needs which are getting in the way of any possible behaviour change.

We then have to consider those 3 key questions from Chapter 1:

What is the UNMET NEED the child is trying to fulfill through this behaviour?

What has this child NOT had experience of?

What is it that this child CANNOT believe about the teacher and the classroom?

FRAMEWORK I WHERE THE FEELINGS COME FROM

It is interesting to note how the teacher is feeling about Megan's behaviour and what information this might give us about how Megan feels. The teacher says he gets a headache, and feels irritated. Maybe that's what it's like in the classroom for Megan; perhaps it's painful and unsettling for her to have so many thoughts flying round in her head, maybe irritating not to know what to focus on first.

FRAMEWORK 2 THE EFFECTS OF TRAUMA ON LEARNING

Just like Lee in Chapter 2, children like Megan haven't learned to trust their relationship with the teacher. But in addition, they haven't learned that it can be safe to focus on just one thing at a time. As mentioned above, their need to be hyper-vigilant may come from living or having lived in a violent, unpredictable environment at home, where it was necessary to keep attention focused outwards on several things at one time. It might also have been learned in an environment which wasn't threatening as such, but just simply chaotic, where the adults themselves constantly switched attention from one thing to another, or there were a lot of children vying for attention. Whatever the cause, these children need to learn what it is like to focus on one thing and 'tune out' distractions. They need to learn that it is possible for their brain to do this. They need to experience the feeling of sitting and thinking about one thing, feeling safe and knowing that they are not in a hostile environment.

So Megan's learning needs can be summarised as follows:
- a need to have an experience of an adult who can remember her, hold her in mind and think about her calmly
- a need to feel safe in the relationship with the teacher, so that she can begin to believe that she doesn't need to be in 'fight/flight/freeze' mode all the time
- a need to learn to soothe her own anxiety and fear about the environment
- a need to trust that she can become absorbed in the task without fear of attack from any direction
- a need to learn how to tune out distractions, 'switch off' some of her concerns, and allow one thought at a time
- like Lee in Chapter 2, a need to be able to trust her own brain to hold important thoughts and remember them
- a need to have the experience of sitting and thinking about one thing,

and then to have the calm feeling of doing this named for her as 'concentration'. She will then recognise what concentration is and what it's like, and be able to get into that state again when necessary

- a need to have a positive experience of the *results* of concentration, so that she gets to know the feeling of satisfaction which comes after effortful absorption

FRAMEWORK 3 ATTACHMENT PATTERN

In attachment terms, we might describe children like Megan as exhibiting an *insecure/ambivalent-resistant* pattern of behaviour. In terms of the Learning Triangle (*see p.29*) these children are constantly checking how safe the environment around them is, particularly relationships, so they can't focus on the task. Constantly running around the class may have been Megan's way of maintaining a predictable relationship with the teacher at all times. The teacher needs to help Megan feel safe enough within her relationship with him, so that she can settle into the task of learning.

FRAMEWORK 4 PLAY DEVELOPMENT

In terms of play development, it would seem that Megan has not learned to play alone or in the presence of others. She is at a very basic stage of development, as she cannot soothe herself by playing quietly. In order to do this, she would need to be able to feel safe from attack. She seems to be operating in a constant state of 'fight or flight'. This would suggest she has rarely or never had the experience of playing with a favourite toy or game, knowing that a caring, supportive adult was nearby to keep her in mind and enjoy her absorption in what she is doing.

REFLECT • RESPOND

Strategies

PLANNING LESSONS TO MANAGE THE NEED

- ✔ Essentially, this child needs to understand it is normal to have a lot of different thoughts and that it is also safe to put some of them 'on hold' in class. You can say something like:

  "It's hard to believe, but it is OK to forget some of your other problems when in class"

  "This classroom is a safe place. I know you find it hard to believe sometimes"

- ✔ You can also try many of strategies used with Lee in Chapter 2 (p.45), particularly those which address anxiety about doing a task alone, without the teacher's immediate presence. The strategies already mentioned are:

  - ✓ set small timed tasks which gradually train Megan to focus for short periods of time, without having to keep checking out the potential dangers in her environment. This can be marked with younger children with egg-timers and older pupils with the clock-face or their own watch

  - ✓ choose tasks which follow a known pattern and are easy to start, so there are fewer chances to get distracted and there is safety in knowing what to do. For example, you might start each task with a review of key words in the form of a word scramble

  - ✓ as with Lee in Chapter 2, reassure Megan that she is not being left to face too many difficulties alone, by saying:

    "Try the first 3 questions on your own and then I will come back and check. I will only be over there"

  - ✓ make sure you do come back, and that if you get distracted, that you acknowledge what has happened: *"I am sorry I did not get back*

> *to you when we agreed, that must have been worrying for you. You probably thought you had been left to do it on your own but I had not forgotten you."*

- ✓ encourage the pupil to trust their own thinking on one topic: *"Take a moment and trust your own brain on this. It's safe to do so. What does it think?"*

✔ Choose activities which are structured and boundaried. For example, putting answers in boxes or drawing frames around answers can help these pupils feel safe and make divisions between different topics. The physical representation on the page seems to help them to understand that they can keep things in boxes in their own minds

✔ Plan to have a bank of soothing left-brain activities such as colouring in, sorting, matching, putting things in order. These pupils will need these types of tasks at times when they are feeling very agitated

PLANNING ACTIVITIES TO HELP DEVELOP SKILLS

✔ Children such as Megan need to practice ways of 'tuning out' what is not relevant to the task. One way of doing this is with a game such as 'Talking in ears' (see p.108).

✔ The 'How long is a minute?' game, described in Chapter 2 (p.45), can also help children who can't focus or bear to wait their turn

(continues…)

🗣 ACTIVITY Talking in ears   (skills development)

Pupils work in teams of five. One pupil sits on a chair and is the 'listener'. The next two pupils sit either side of the listener. The remaining two pupils sit in front, facing the listener. These two pupils have to ask the listener questions on a topic given to them by the teacher. The listener has to listen and answer all the questions put to them. The pupils who are sitting either side of the listener have the task of trying to distract the listener. They do this by talking directly into the listener's ear about a different topic. For example, the questioners might ask questions about a topic from the class curriculum. At the same time, the 'distracters' might talk into the ears about their best holiday.

Give the pupils a chance to experience each role. Ask for feedback on what it was like to be the listener and what strategies the pupils were using to focus on the questions and block out the distractions. Explain that this is what is needed sometimes in class to keep focused. Pupils will usually want to repeat the exercise and try different strategies to focus. Pupils with poor focus can learn from their peers. Peers can also learn how difficult it is for some pupils to block out distractions.

Teachers can refer back to the learning from the game when there are moments of not being able to focus. You might say, for example: *"Remember what it was like when we played the 'Talking in Ears' game, and you were being asked all the questions, remember what it was like to focus only on that and ignore the other people? That's what you need to do now"*

Using metaphor to understand what is happening in the brain

Children such as Megan need to realise they can control their own brains and take some responsibility for their own thinking. Asking the child Clean Language* questions to elicit a metaphor for her experience can help everyone in the class. This kind of metaphor work is also useful when done with the whole class to encourage them to get into good states for learning and to understand how to focus better. For example, Clean Language Questions can be asked to elicit a good state for learning at the start of a class. The following is an example from a twelve year old girl.

Teacher "If this class was going to be the best for you for learning, it would be like what?"

Jenny "Like a lovely, clear river which you can swim in"

Teacher "And that's a lovely, clear river, like what?"

Jenny "A lovely, warm, blue, clear river which is safe"

Teacher "And that's a lovely, warm, blue, clear river and safe like what?"

Jenny "Safe like no-one will jump in and disturb you"

The basic question of *"That's a ... like what"* can be asked a few times until the pupil has created a strong metaphor, usually three or four times is enough. You'll recognise when to stop, because the same image will keep recurring. The pupils can ask each other these questions and then draw their metaphor for learning at their best. These can be displayed in the classroom or kept at the front of their books. By creating a metaphor for a good state for learning, they will get into that state and be more ready and able to learn.

Clean Language is an approach for helping people explore their own metaphors for issues and problems, developed in the 1980's by psychotherapist David Groves. The key to Clean Language is asking questions which do not impose the questioner's view or interpretation on the client's metaphor. The key question used in Clean Language is "And that's a... like.what?". In my work with children in an informal setting, I sometimes find it helpful to change this to the question, "What's that like?" (see Lawley & Tompkins, 2000 and www. cleanlanguage.co.uk for more information).

ELICITING A METAPHOR

The teacher can ask:

> "Megan, what's it like when you
> can't focus?"

In my experience, children like Megan say something along the lines of:

> "It's like having all the lights in a house
> on and not knowing what room
> to go into"

The next question would be:

Teacher "What would need to happen in order to know what room to go into?"

Megan "Some lights would have to be switched off"

Teacher "How can you do that?"

Megan "I'll go round and switch them off"

Teacher "Can you do that?"

Megan "Yes"

The teacher then decides to say:

> "Switch off all the lights in your mind
> and open the ones to do with this
> lesson. What's that like?"

Megan "OK, like being at home and staying in one room to watch TV"

Teacher "OK, can you stay in that one room and imagine you are doing your work? That's like what"?

Megan "Like everything else isn't important"

Teacher "OK, that's what we call focusing on one thing. I want you to do that now. Imagine all the other lights have been switched off and you are just in this room. That's like what?"

At this point, the pupil might tell you something about what stops him using this strategy successfully. That's not a problem if you continue to work with the metaphor.

Megan "I'm worried I can never go in the other room"

Teacher "OK, that's worried like what?"

Megan "Like I'm worried that I need someone to tell me that I'll be able to go in there at other times and that I'm not missing something important or dangerous"

Teacher "And can you tell yourself that"?

Megan "Yes, that's OK, cool"

Once the pupil has developed a metaphor, you can mention it to them to bring them back to focusing. For example:

> "OK, Megan, I think you need to put
> those other lights out now".

If you can give Megan some individual time, you can work with her to explore the metaphor and to help her notice when it's working better. You can also help her work out how she can remind herself to turn off those other lights, if she notices she's beginning to get distracted.

III   PLANNING OUTSIDE THE CLASS

✓ If Megan can have individual time outside class with a supportive adult, she will benefit from work on activities which serve to externalise some of the internal anxieties which may be ruling her thoughts.

Activities which help with this could be:

✓ Spaceship drawing - ask the child to draw a spaceship and imagine she is going on a journey for about a year into space. Inside the spaceship, ask her to draw what she would take with her and what it should look like. Allow her free rein. Stay in the metaphor and discuss her drawings with her. This metaphor gives the child the opportunity to explore, among other things, ideas about independence (who does she take with her?), caring for herself (does she take food?), security (does she put in safety devices?), control (who is in charge of the ship?) and generally what it is like in her own special space for thinking

✓ Stick figure dialogues - draw a stick person - boy or girl depending on who you are working with - and ask the pupil to complete the drawing. Use a speech bubble and ask her to imagine what the person is saying. Then draw a thought bubble and ask her to imagine what the person is thinking. Point out that what we say and what we think are not always the same. You can develop this into dialogues between people, and stories. This often gives children the chance to voice secret anxieties and thoughts.

You'll know that a kid who can't sit still is making progress when ...

★ you don't notice her every five minutes

★ she is NOT constantly getting up and wandering around (in fact, improvement will mostly consist of what she is NOT doing. It is important to acknowledge her when she is behaving appropriately, since, when you're not speaking to her every five minutes, it's easy to overlook other kinds of progress)

★ you feel focused in a lesson with her and not constantly distracted or irritated by her behaviour

★ she can finish the tasks set without someone sitting glued to her side to keep her in her seat

★ her body language shows you that she is feeling calm, settled and relaxed

Chapter 7

"What can I do with the kid who… can't remember anything?"

Brian is fourteen and seems unable to follow simple instructions or to retain information. His teacher says,

> "Brian is a pleasant boy but he seems totally scatty. He needs every instruction repeated several times and often acts as if he's never heard of something which we only did the day before. He seems totally unable to remember facts and information, but I wonder sometimes if it's just an act. I think he might just be lazy. He lies about his behaviour, and won't admit if he's done something wrong, even if he's been caught out or observed by someone else. When you try to talk about it, he says "Dunno", or stares at you vacantly. There is a kind of delayed reaction to everything you ask him. It's as if he's in a world of his own."

A pupil in his class says,

> "Brian is a complete idiot. He pretends he doesn't hear the teacher and everyone has to wait ages for him to answer questions. We all end up shouting at him to hurry up and stop being such a pain."

Using the RETHINK model for thinking about Brian

We can see from the above description that Brian's behaviour is not providing an outright challenge to the teacher, but is irritating and time-consuming and preventing Brian from progressing in his learning. He is also annoying his classmates, and his behaviour is impeding the flow of the lesson.

STAGE I *REVIEW*

We can begin by focusing on what's happening in the class at the moment for Brian, **reviewing** any interventions already in place. Have Brian's learning needs been assessed, for example? The teacher is interpreting his behaviour as 'lazy': but has he ever been assessed by an Educational Psychologist? Children like Brian may be dyslexic, have a hearing problem or another learning difficulty which has somehow been missed.

As a classroom teacher, we can also take a step back and observe what happens when Brian doesn't answer or can't seem to remember.

Is he left alone and not challenged to answer, as it takes so long to get him to understand? Does the teacher become impatient and decide it's better to move on without him? Has the teacher practically stopped involving the student in the lesson at all? Brian says,

> *"I don't usually have to read out in the class, 'coz when the teacher gets to me, he usually gets fed up waiting and says,"Don't worry Brian", and moves on to the next person. Some teachers don't even ask me. I'm glad when that happens, because I hate reading".*

Brian's comments indicate that a pattern has been set up which is allowing him to be passed over, to opt out of the lesson and ultimately not learn to read better. We need to think about how activities are set up and how instructions are given: Brian may be missing some very important information at this stage of the lesson, and is then unable to proceed. Are instructions, for example, given at a non-verbal level as well as a verbal? Are they clearly demonstrated, with the teacher giving an example of what to do and then getting an example from the students of what is expected? Is it clear to other students what to do, or do they ask questions at the beginning of a task which show they were not sure about the instructions? Does Brian respond better to written or spoken instructions? What about his learning style?

Can he show he remembers what is being taught when he has to *do* something rather than *say* something? Does he respond better to visuals, diagrams as instructions? How many times does he have to hear something before it is clear? Is it a problem with getting started, keeping going when stuck, or completing? Does he understand and see the point of what is going on?

We also need to **review** the level of the work. Can Brian do the work? Is he in the right level of class? How do you know? What evidence do you really have of this? We can **review** our seating plan. Is he sitting near anyone who is maybe distracting him, or making him anxious?

We can choose to focus on what is working and notice what happens then. What is he like in other lessons, and, if he does remember things, what are the factors which help? What are the *times* when Brian remembers things? For example, he manages to turn up for school, most lessons, and most outside-class clubs on time. How does he do this? Is it because other students help him, or there is a set routine which does not happen in the rest of the class? We could ask him!

REVIEW • RESPOND

Strategies

By choosing to **review** the above, some clear teaching strategies are likely to emerge. We might realise we need to do some or all of the following:

✔ Make sure our instructions are very clear, and given step-by-step in both verbal and non-verbal ways. Check instructions by giving an example of what to do and getting an example from the students. Do the first example together

✔ Experiment with different teaching styles or tasks. Try to include some kinaesthetic activities in the lesson to find out if this student responds better. For example, sometimes give students the opportunity to move around and ask questions: cut up key pieces of information and do matching activities which involve physically putting the pieces back together: have students revise using cards with questions on one side and answers on the other

✔ Sit Brian with different students if you think he's anxious in some groupings

✔ Sit Brian near the front of the class where he can see and hear what's going on

✔ Get an official assessment of his learning needs

✔ Ask Brian *"When you remember things like extra football practice, how do you remember that?"* Use Clean Language to explore this further, so that Brian can develop a metaphor for remembering - *"That's like what?"* Ask *"What's it like when you do remember? How do you do that?"* *(For more on Clean Language see Chapter 6, p.109)*

✔ Work on memory strategies with the class. Encourage a state of curiosity in all your students about how they learn and remember things. Build in activities which help develop memory

✔ Make use of index cards to help students develop memory skills. For example, put questions one side, answers on another. Use the cards for tests, games and quizzes, games such as fill in the gap (gap on one side, word on the other), true/false, translations of words and definitions, multiple choice and so on. Encourage students to take 3 or 4 cards home and get into the habit of looking at them each day. Simple activities like these demonstrate that memory can be developed by *'little-and-often'* practice.

🏠 ACTIVITY Memory Strategy (practice/revision)

Make a list of important facts or events that you want students to remember. Ask students to draw their room or their house. Then ask them to put the facts or events in places in the room or house which makes sense to them (for example, a student might put a quadratic equation formula on his TV in his bedroom, as he knows he needs to view it frequently in order to remember it). Explain that there are no right and wrong answers, that this is to help them develop their brains. Some associations might seem strange to you, but they only need to make sense to the student. Put the students into pairs. Ask them to describe their drawing to their partner. Ask their partners to then repeat back what they have been told whilst the student closes their eyes and imagines going around the house or room putting the things in place. In a follow-up lesson, ask students to recall their drawings, and the events or facts. Discuss other ways of doing this, such a visualising a path with each fact or event representing something found along the way, located within a favourite place and so on.

STAGE 2 *REFRAME*

Assessing Brian's learning needs and paying attention to our classroom management and teaching style might result in him remembering more in the lesson. However, for some pupils, this won't be enough. We need to find other ways to **reframe** the meaning of our interactions with him. In the first instance, we can choose to notice more specifically the point at which Brian 'freezes', and separate this out completely from our interpretation of the *meaning* of this behaviour. For example, the teacher might notice that:

DESCRIPTION	INTERPRETATIONS AND FEELINGS
"When Brian has to read aloud without preparation time, he sits, gazing out the window, and says nothing	*...which makes me **think** he isn't paying any attention or doesn't care*
When I say Brian's name and then ask him a question, he just looks at me for a long time and then asks me to repeat the question several times	*...which makes me **think** he doesn't listen*
When Brian is asked to do a task with a group, he usually sits, laughing and joking, doing no work	*...which makes me **think** he's really lazy"*

This separation of description and behaviour might begin to show us where some of Brian's problems lie. There appear to be trigger points: if the teacher can move away from her interpretations, she might begin to see he has problems around confidence with reading, hearing or even interaction with peers.

Secondly, we could **reframe** the teacher's reactions to Brian's 'slowness'. She appears to be drawn into wanting him to hurry up, to give the right answer and move on. This could be an example of a teacher being caught up in *transference*, where she's unintentionally re-enacting an adult role with which Brian is familiar. Her impatience may be information about Brian's previous interactions with key adults in his life (*see below, and for more on transference, see p.91*). Whether that's true or not, we need to make sure we stay in our teaching role, and use the opportunity to develop Brian's learning skills.

Finally, we could also **reframe** Brian's behaviour by looking for a postive intention in it. What message is it conveying to us? Perhaps he's showing us that he doesn't want to interrupt the flow of our teaching with his inability to answer, and that he doesn't want to hold the rest of the class back. If we choose to believe this, we'll see his silence not as laziness, but as co-operation!

REFRAME • RESPOND
Strategies

- ✔ Notice if you're being drawn into acting a certain role with pupils such as Brian. Do something to break the pattern of interaction
- ✔ Practise patience! Allow the silence to last a little longer than you are comfortable with. You may be surprised at the outcome, and, whatever happens, you'll learn more about Brian (and possibly yourself!) than if you fill the silence with your own suggestions
- ✔ Act as if there's a positive intention in Brian's behaviour, and, if appropriate, name it for him:
  "It's OK if we stop and take some time on this, it could be helpful to everyone"

STAGE 3 *REFLECT*
Reflect on the pupil's needs and feelings

With some students, the strategies and comments outlined above may be enough for them to start responding more appropriately. However, if the behaviour persists, it may be showing us that this student has some unmet need which is driving the apparent memory difficulties. So then we need to consider those 3 key questions from Chapter 1.

What is the UNMET NEED the child is trying to fulfill through this behaviour?

What has this child NOT had experience of?

What is it that this child CANNOT believe about the teacher and the classroom?

FRAMEWORK 1 WHERE THE FEELINGS COME FROM

It is interesting to notice that the other pupils think Brian is an idiot and the teacher believes he is lazy and not interested. Perhaps Brian himself often feels stupid in class. The pupils' reactions might be an example of the unconscious defence mechanism of *projection*: they may be voicing what is going on in Brian's head *("I'm useless, I'm too slow, I'm an idiot",* for example). Similarly, the teachers appear to be unable to think constructively about Brian's problems: they judge him as 'not being bothered'. In effect, they are pushing the issue of his learning needs away from themselves. Perhaps they are also feeling stupid, and unable to think of solutions *(for more on projection, see Chapter 3).* Brian can't believe that it's possible for him to trust his own thinking, and it appears that the teachers are also becoming blocked in their thinking around how to work with him. Brian needs to learn that the adults have the capacity to think about him and create new learning strategies, and that they won't give up on him. He may not have had an experience of this in his early years.

FRAMEWORK 2 THE EFFECTS OF TRAUMA ON LEARNING

Although as classroom teachers we may not know much about Brian's background, we can try to think about how early traumatic experiences might have affected his ability to retain information. Brian might be an example of a child who has not had experience of an adult who is able to think about him, remember him and hold onto him in their mind. He may have been able to develop little sense of his own history and life because he hasn't had a caring adult to give him a 'script', that is, to tell stories and anecdotes about his past. We learn to think by being remembered and thought about, and children such as Brian may not have had this opportunity. In chaotic, violent situations, for example, the adult, for whatever reason, has no capacity to remember a child's needs. The child can quite literally 'fall' from the adult's minds, in the same way that Brian now says *"Stuff just falls out my brain"*. It can also happen where the child has had multiple foster placements. In fact, Brian's new social worker says:

> *"You should see Brian's file, it's impossible to keep track of all the placements and schools he's been to: pieces of paper fall out of it all the time, nothing is in order, it's a right mess".*

Tragically, this is not uncommon for children such as Brian: it's no wonder he finds it hard to keep his own memory in good working order. In addition, Brian may have childhood memories which are too scary or sad to remember, and his block about learning could be a defensive response to not wanting to be overwhelmed by huge, unmanageable feelings. Traumatic losses, deaths and separations can all trigger this kind of response.

FRAMEWORK 3 ATTACHMENT PATTERN

Brian doesn't appear to be able to make use of the relationship with teaching staff or to 'do the task' of learning. He may be exhibiting a form of *insecure/disorganised* attachment pattern (*see p.28*). Children who have lived in constant fear of abuse and violence or who have had multiple traumatic upheavals in their lives can show this behaviour in class. The oldest part of their brain is being activated in response to perceiving constant threat and in Brian's case, it is the response of 'freeze' which is most apparent. Like Peter in Chapter 5, Brian's brain has stuck on an almost automated, programmed response to living in unpredictable chaos but, unlike Peter whose response is aggression ('fight'), Brian's response is to stand still, not move and hope the threat goes away ('freeze'). School needs to be a safe, predictable structure, which allows these children an unthreatening space where they are thought about, and where their anxieties can be contained to some extent so that they can learn.

FRAMEWORK 4 PLAY DEVELOPMENT

It's possible that Brian hasn't had any experience of playing with an adult or with someone who plays by the rules. Children like Brian often play games as if there are no patterns and no rules, or as if they can't remember them, thus annoying the other children. He may not have had the experience of sitting in a relaxed way and having the time to make mistakes, take risks and see how a game works. If Brian has experienced several moves from foster placement to foster placement, for example, he may have found it difficult to join in with the play of yet more new children. If the Brian in your class has had no experience of the shared space of playing, he will find it hard to learn in class. He will need a chance to play and learn in a structured, repetitive way, to take things apart and put them back together in order to understand that games operate on a logical level.

By looking at what is happening with Brian through the four frameworks, we can see that Brian's needs are:

- to have a calm, safe, structured thinking experience with a caring adult who can help him to name his feelings, particularly his underlying anxieties, and help him make some sense of his past experience. This might mean having some individual work with an appropriate person, such as the school counsellor or a Learning Mentor with counselling skills

- to have enough repeated experiences of this type of thinking to help 'unfreeze' his learned response to his fear of learning (going blank and switching off)

- to learn to trust the relationship with an adult, and not expect it to be either abusive or taken away suddenly

- to learn to take risks, try out learning and make mistakes without fear of humiliation
- to learn to trust his own thinking
- to learn some strategies for trusting his memory

REFLECT • RESPOND

Strategies

I   LESSON PLANNING

✔ Build 'learning to learn' and memory strategies into your lessons

✔ Use games which can be repeated and used for reviewing different topics.
For example, make your own jigsaw activity for revision of any key subjects

✂ ACTIVITY Jigsaw   (revision activity)

Divide a piece of A4 paper into eight squares. On each side of a square,
write a question and on the side of the adjoining square, write the answer.
For example, if you are doing simple maths multiplication revision you would

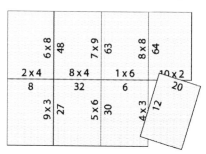

write your sum - 6 x 8 - on the right hand
edge of one square and the answer, 48, on
the left hand edge of the adjoining square.
Thus each square will have a sum on each
side of its line. You can also put sums
above and below the horizontal line.

Cut up the paper into the 8 squares. Students then put the paper back
together by matching the sums with the answer.

This can be used for other subjects, such as words and translations in French,
cities and capitals in geography, events and dates in history, chemicals and
their symbols for science.

II   PLANNING ON THE SPOT RESPONSES

✓ Essentially, these pupils need to learn to trust their own thinking. So plan to say things which help them to do this, for example:

"Maybe you find it hard to believe that you can remember: take a moment to think, and trust your own brain. How do you think you spell …?". (If the pupil gets it wrong, encourage them to see this as information about which bit they need to re-learn)

✓ They then need to know what it is like to be sure and to trust that feeling of 'knowing'. Get into the habit of encouraging self-checking when they do give you a correct answer. Teach them to recognise that feeling of knowing by checking where it is in their bodies. *"You know this, notice how that feels and where that feeling of knowing is inside you"*

✓ Ask *"… Are you sure? How do you know you are sure?"* The pupil will usually give a short response such as *"I just know"*, or *"It feels right"*. The latter is all you are looking for at this stage, as it is a sign the pupil is developing an internal checking mechanism

✓ Make sure that you acknowledge progress to them. It's not a mistake to know that you are not sure, and that you feel something about the fact or memory you have in your mind is wrong: it's progress in the process of learning to self-monitor

✓ Be prepared to acknowledge any mistakes you make yourself, or anything you don't remember. This shows the student that making mistakes and forgetting are part of being human

✓ If they are convinced they can never remember anything, use a 'carrot' in a humorous way. I have found it useful to say, *"Would you remember if you knew I was going to give you five pounds? How would you help yourself remember that?"*

✓ Name what you think might be happening in their brain. *"Maybe your brain is full up of stuff and you find it hard to remember"*

Name the anxiety if appropriate: *"Sometimes we don't want to remember, it's too difficult to remember some things"*

✔ Be aware of any projection, and name it if appropriate: *"I'm feeling a bit stuck now, I wonder if you are? Sometimes we feel stupid when we can't do something really quickly, and that's a normal feeling to have"*

✔ Be aware of what might be happening for other students and address it (if appropriate - it may not always be good to draw attention to their responses) *"Rushing through things is not always the best way to learn, and sometimes it's good for us all to be more patient and see what happens when we slow down a bit"*

✔ Above all, allow time and thinking space, rather than rushing through things or passing over the 'Brian' in your class simply because you are not able to bear the anxiety of waiting for him to answer

III   PLANNING FOR OUTSIDE CLASS

This child will benefit greatly from some individual time with a caring adult who has some counselling skills. This person should use the time to focus on developing the skills described above and addressing the emotional aspects of learning, rather than completing classroom or homework tasks with the child.

✔ Use activities which allow Brian to sort out his own timeline and school history with a caring adult. For example, just asking him to help you put some major events in his life in order can be a good beginning. You can start with the different schools he's been to, and the years he went to them. This keeps it safer for him than encouraging him to look at family events. You might need to do this several times before he can make sense of his moves

👍 ACTIVITY   The confidence bracelet: learning skills
(warm up)

This is a variation of an NLP* activity which can be useful to teach to students to help them access positive states for learning and remembering. Ask students to think of a time they remembered something well. It can be quite a simple thing, such as always coming to class on time. Students like Brian might find it difficult to think of a example, so you can do this activity after you have played a game where they did remember something. Say to students,

"See the time in your mind: hear what you were hearing, feel what you were feeling. Take the feeling and imagine I am turning it up, as we do with a radio or ipod: that's right, really feel the feeling".

Ask students to imagine a circle on the floor in front of them and, when they are ready, to step into it and take the feeling with them. When they are in their circles, tell them to feel the feeling in their whole body and to choose a word to say to themselves to remember this feeling. Then tell them to step out of the circle and imagine it can be picked up and put on their wrist as a bracelet. They should do this and put the bracelet on their wrist by encircling one wrist with their finger and thumb. Tell students that this 'confidence bracelet' is on their wrists now, and when they want to remember something, before trying to do so, they should hold their wrist, say the word and bring the feeling back.

This will seem crazy to some students (and some teachers!), but it works!

*NLP is Neuro-Linguistic Programming, a model of communication developed in the 1970's by Richard Bandler and Michael Grinder, based on analysing what excellent communicators seem to have in common: what they believe about themselves and others, how they behave and the precise language patterns they use. For further information, see McDermott & O'Connor (1996). For applications to teaching see Terry and Churches, (2008).

✔ If possible, get the child involved in a quiet lunchtime games club which will allow him to have a calm space and to learn to take some safe risks. For example, a board games club can be a lot of fun and develops important skills

✔ If you can give this child some individual time to work on his metaphors for learning and remembering, it will help greatly (see p.109)

When working with a Learning Mentor, one child who was falling behind and finding it hard to remember at school came up with the following metaphor for her brain. The mentor asked her,

Learning Mentor	"What just happened in your brain?"
Nancy	"It went to sleep"
Learning Mentor	"And that's went to sleep like what?"
Nancy	"Like going down here… (*child points to bottom of throat*) … and going to sleep because he's tired"
Learning Mentor	"And that's tired like what?"
Nancy	"Tired like he needs a rest and doesn't want to work any more"
Learning Mentor	"And how could he wake up after his rest?"
Nancy	"I'll just tell him to go back"
Learning Mentor	"Can you do that?"
Nancy	"Yes" … and she continued on with her work!

The Learning Mentor was able to help the child use the metaphor herself, and also passed it on as a strategy for teachers to use as a way of talking to the child when they noticed she was 'switching off'.

✔ As with other students in this book, stories which address their particular internal anxieties can be very helpful as discussion points, for example, 'Teenie Weenie in a Too Big World' (Sunderland, 2003) (*for a discussion of the use of stories of this nature with older children, please see p.77*)

You'll know the kid who can't remember is making progess when …

★ he remembers something, particularly if it means admitting to a mistake or wrong doing!

★ he wants to be included in the classroom plenary or points out you are missing him out

★ he can bear to have a go and get something wrong

★ he loses the 'rabbit trapped in the headlights' look when asked to recall something

★ you feel as if you might sometimes be on the same planet!

Chapter 8

"What can I do with the kid who… controls the classroom?"

Nikki is fifteen. She is bright and has the ability to do well in her exams. Her teachers, however, find her very challenging, and at times they admit it's difficult to even like her. Her maths teacher says,

> *"The trouble with Nikki is that you can't tell her anything: she knows it all, and wants to do everything on her own terms. She's always disrupting the lesson by insisting we do something different and often, when she doesn't get her own way, she refuses to do the work , either doing something else on her own or spending the lesson chatting and winding up the others. She's a real ringleader in the class, and loves to get the others off-task if she's not interested".*

Other teachers think Nikki is just *"spoilt and arrogant"*. They often say that *"she has to learn that she can't have it all her own way"*. Nikki says,

> *"I think I'm doing alright in school. I don't know what their problem is. I get good grades and get my work done. It's not my problem if the others don't get their work done".*

Using the RETHINK model to think about Nikki

STAGE 1   *REVIEW*

1   CLASSROOM MANAGEMENT

When we look at what's happening in class, it would appear that Nikki is actually interested in learning, but doesn't seem to care about the group needs. All her teachers agree that she does get her work completed to a high standard. The difficulty they're having is the effect on the group when Nikki doesn't follow instructions. She's an independent learner; she needs to see the point in what she's learning and why she's doing it. In addition, once she's engaged in something, Nikki finds it difficult to stop work on that particular task until she's finished it to her satisfaction. One teacher says:

> *"It is almost as if she's obsessed once she gets interested in a topic. She just can't let it drop and will keep on with it, even if we need to move onto the next thing"*

We might also notice that this method has brought Nikki success so far, so she's unlikely to change it just because the teacher tells her to!

REVIEW • RESPOND

Strategies

✔ Work with the student's learning style. If you can see beyond the power struggle with this pupil, you may be able to get her interested in how she learns. Use a learning style quiz to involve her in discovering her preferred style and use this information to plan lessons

✔ Include some self-directed study in your lessons

✔ Praise her for completed work and encourage her independent learning. It shouldn't become a challenge

STAGE 2 **REFRAME**

There is a lot of judgment in the teacher's comments. We need to begin our **reframe** by separating out Nikki's behaviour from our judgments about it, so that we're clear what we're dealing with. As teachers, we often find it difficult to like students who seem to be in control of the class, because *we* need to be in control! It's easy to be pulled into arguments and power struggles with the 'Nikkis' in our classes. They are adept at drawing the teacher into discussions about why she is teaching a certain way, or what she's doing.

We could **reframe** Nikki's need for control as her need to be in charge of her own learning. This is actually a very positive learning trait if we can harness it and work with it (*as above*). Moreover, saying a pupil *"... knows what she's doing and is in control all the time"* is not the same as saying *"She needs to feel in control"*. The former suggests that the pupil is deliberately trying to take control of the class, whereas if we identify this pattern as an unconscious need, perhaps developed as a result of life circumstances, we can view the child more favourably.

Another way to **reframe** this interaction is to pay attention to your own feelings and ask yourself what this pupil might be triggering in you. Your own desire to stay in control of this situation could be symptomatic of other things being or feeling out of control for you, in the classroom, in the school in general, or in your own life. Although we do need to feel in charge of our classrooms, we shouldn't feel an overwhelming need to control every last thing about our students. We need to be able to meet them in a co-operative learning space. Nikki's reluctance to let the teacher have power over her, or her fear of this happening, can somehow result in teachers wanting to *over*-exert their influence. When Nikki's maths teacher thought about this issue, he realised:

"I was having a really hard time with my head of department, I felt like nothing was under control: it made me very anxious with exams coming

up. I realised I was displacing that anxiety; I was trying extra hard to control my classes, because I couldn't control my workload".

REFRAME • RESPOND

Strategies

✔ Describe the behaviour and your interpretation of it to the pupil

"When you carry on with something even though I've asked you to stop, it makes it difficult to teach the rest of the class. I need you to stop when asked, so that we can all learn as well as possible"

✔ If the pupil is a successful but independent learner, build in some element of choice to activities. For example, if there are two tasks, give some choice in the order they can be completed

✔ Acknowledge her strengths and explain why it's necessary to work with the group sometimes

"I know you are very good at learning on your own: we also need to work on this together this lesson, so I can be clear everyone understands"

✔ Avoid the temptation to use a power approach such as:

"I am the teacher here, not you" or

"This lesson can't be only about you". This provokes unnecessary conflict. Stick to the primary aim of learning. If you need to reinforce your position as the teacher, do it by focusing on the task

"This task is very important for the exam. We all need to look at it now so that I can be sure you all know what to do".

✔ Be aware of your own personal situation and what this pupil might be triggering in you. Deal with this separately to the pupil's behaviour

STAGE 3 *REFLECT*

If we have **reframed** what Nikki is doing, we can take some time to **reflect** on this core issue of control. We then have to consider those 3 key questions from Chapter 1:

> **What is the UNMET NEED the child is trying to fulfill through this behaviour?**
>
> **What has this child NOT had experience of?**
>
> **What is it that this child CANNOT believe about the teacher and the classroom?**

FRAMEWORK I WHERE THE FEELINGS COME FROM

Nikki's need for control could be seen as an example of *omnipotence*. Omnipotence is an unconscious defence mechanism which can come in to play when we feel threatened or out of control. Children try to keep control of their environment by acting as if they are all-powerful and need no-one. This defence often occurs when a child has had loss or sudden trauma in their early years. There have been catastrophes, and the child had no control over them. In later years, their defence may be to keep everything under control and act as if they 'know everything'. They cannot bear not knowing.

FRAMEWORK 2 EFFECTS OF TRAUMA ON LEARNING

We need to look at what might have led this specific student to have such an overwhelming need to be in control. Why, for example, does Nikki find it so difficult to disengage from a task once she's involved in it? The kind of catastrophic events described above may have left pupils such as Nikki with powerful feelings of abandonment and vulnerability. It is also likely that, for whatever reason, caring and supportive adults were not available to deal with the child's overwhelming sense of loss. This left the child with an almost obsessive desire to take control of their own life and activities. So tasks can seem very safe for these children, hence their desire to remain engaged with projects until they are completed. Tasks which aren't yet finished can feel threatening, because they can introduce a sense of uncertainty about things unravelling, things getting lost, things being fuzzy, not completely known or controllable. Complete closure is safer.

Allowing an adult to take control can also seem threatening, if Nikki's experience has been that adults can't be trusted to cope. Asking her to do what you say implies she should hand over control to you; where might that put her? Maybe in a place too vulnerable to bear, if you inadvertently let her down or miss her anxiety.

We could therefore identify Nikki's needs as:

- a need to learn to allow the adults to be adults, and to trust that they will be able to sustain this role
- a need for the teachers therefore to show they can act like adults
- a need to realise that catastrophes are not around every corner, that things can be left unfinished between lessons, and that they will still be there in the next lesson
- a need to learn that it's safe to ask for help, because Nikki's intelligence will only get her to a certain standard, and she needs to learn how to ask in order to really excel

FRAMEWORK 3 ATTACHMENT PATTERN

Nikki would seem to be exhibiting an *insecure/avoidant* attachment pattern. Her focus is on the task, and not the relationship. The teacher, by trying to dominate the relationship, is doing what the pupil finds hard and doesn't trust. The answer - as with other children with this pattern - will primarily come from working through the task and focusing on the learning.

FRAMEWORK 4 PLAY DEVELOPMENT

Children such as Nikki haven't learned to play by other people's rules or, alternatively, they might have learned to do this at an early age, but loss or trauma has caused them to revert to their own rules. Games led by others can't be trusted: they may seem or be too dangerous or risky.

REFLECT • RESPOND

Strategies

- ✔ Work on the child's need to focus on task, but show that a co-operative relationship is not dangerous
- ✔ Keep work safe. These pupils often have very averse reactions to being told that you have forgotten to bring their work into school, or that their work has gone missing. Be organised in your collecting and storing of work
- ✔ Have regular but also flexible routines. It may help to sometimes give a bit of leeway in the way a task is done, if it keeps learning on track
- ✔ If something does go wrong, acknowledge it
- ✔ Be aware if you're arguing for the sake of it, and keep focused on the learning goal
- ✔ Keep the pupil focused on her future, because this will help develop a shared goal. The student is working towards achieving a positive future for herself and your lesson can be seen as providing a route. You are on the path together, not in opposition to each other
- ✔ Work alongside the pupil, not against her: be careful that you don't find yourself opposing requests from this child just to show you have power over her. Enlist her opinions about her learning
- ✔ See beyond the 'all-knowing' facade to the vulnerable child within
- ✔ Name some of the anxieties she may be experiencing. For example, *"It's*

hard to trust people to do it properly, but you can." "Getting help doesn't mean you're no good yourself." "Some of us find it hard to let others help us. We think they won't do it right"

II   PLANNING TO DEVELOP SKILLS

✔ These pupils find it hard to show empathy to others. They have built up defences which focus totally on their own needs and goals. If possible, include some activities which encourage them to develop empathy and see the world from another's point of view.

👄 ACTIVITY 'I'll answer for you'
(empathy/ice-breakers/energisers)

Students work in groups of four. One student sits on a chair and two students stand behind her. The fourth student asks questions to the student on the chair. They should be questions about the student - their likes/dislikes, and so on. The student on the chair remains silent and the two standing behind have to answer the questions for her, trying to imagine what her answers would be. The student on the chair simply nods or shakes her head to indicate how accurate the answers are. The students take turns in the different positions. This game is an excellent practice of the skill of empathy, *'walking in someone else's shoes'.* It can also show students how they come across to others. The content of the questions can be changed to reflect topics being taught, but the basic skill of empathy is the main focus (it's important to put a few boundaries around the type of questions which can be asked, to ensure they don't become too intrusive).

🗨️ACTIVITY Reverse role play   (empathy)

Choose a situation which students need to practise or review. Put the students into pairs. Give them the situation and explain that they are going to perform a role play. Give them the roles. Tell them that when you clap your hands, they should freeze in whatever position they are in. Get them started on the role play. Clap your hands. Tell students to notice their partner's position and then to swap positions. Explain that when you clap your hands again, they should continue the role play but from the new position (ie taking the other student's part). Clap your hands. Get students to change positions at least twice more.

This activity allows students to experience an argument or event from two different viewpoints, which helps to develop the skill of empathy with others and more acceptance of difference and diversity.

III   PLANNING FOR OUTSIDE CLASS

✔ View Nikki's need to be in control as a leadership quality. Train her to be a peer mentor, or to support a younger pupil in a topic or field she's good at

✔ Share your ideas about behaviour and what drives it.

Give her extra resources to read and look at, to form her own opinion

⊞ ACTIVITY   Backs to the board
(review of vocabulary/concepts)

Students work in small groups. They take it in turns to come to the board. One student (A) sits with his or her back to the board, and the other four or five students sit in a line facing the board. The teacher writes a key word, definition or piece of information on the board. The other students have to get the student with their back to the board to say the exact word(s). They can say anything except for any part of the word or information.

When student (A) works out what the word is, everyone changes round, and another student has their back to the board. The aim is to see how many items can be got right within time-limits, such as two minutes or so. Then another group comes to the board.

This game develops a lot of skills - listening, explaining so that someone else can understand, working as a group, and learning to work together.

You'll know that a kid who controls the class is making progress when ...

★ *she can allow the teacher's agenda to take precedence most of the time*

★ *she is prepared to use her ability to control to help the teacher or other students*

★ *she starts work faster, without arguing about why it needs to be done, in that way or at that time*

★ *she asks you for help or seems to value something you've said*

★ *she can have fun making a fool of herself in a more relaxed and unstructured way, for example on a school charity fundraising day*

Chapter 9

"What can I do with the parent/carer who …?"

Working with challenges from parents/carers

When dealing with pupils who challenge us, it's also very important to try to work in co-operation with their parents/carers. We can see that all the children in this book need consistency of care and approach in order to develop the skills needed for classroom learning. If school and home can co-operate to provide reasonably consistent care, children will realise that common boundaries exist, and learning can happen in both places. Of course this is the ideal scenario, and we know that many children live in chaotic environments where school is not a priority. Even in these cases, if we persevere with meetings with the parent/carer, we will at the very least get additional information to help us in our dealings with our pupils. Liasing with families can be complex, time-consuming and frustrating, but it can also save us time and reduce our frustration by giving us extra and important insights.

Why it can be difficult

In my experience, few of us receive training on how to deal with parents and in particular, how to manage meetings with the parents of children who challenge us. In a workshop recently, a head of year from a secondary school said,

> *"I know we're supposed to be able to work closely with the parents, but no-one really tells you how to do it. I got a bit of advice from the deputy*

head when I began seeing parents more often, but mostly I had to just muddle along. I manage quite well with most of my pupils, and with meetings such as parents' evening, but I still struggle at times with those meetings with parents of kids who are constantly in trouble. If I'm honest, I find myself either blaming them, or feeling sorry for them and then worrying that I can't help them".

So, although it is generally agreed that this kind of work is essential, staff in school - even the most senior - are rarely trained in how to deal with difficult situations with parents/carers. Pastoral staff usually say that they just use their own commonsense and experience, and that some people are just *'better with parents than others'*. That may be true, but, as with working with the kids, we can all improve our skills for managing challenging situations and meetings.

The feelings in the room

Moreover, we should remember that, as Sue Pantner says,

> It must be recognised that the area of pupil behaviour is highly emotive. It challenges teachers' sense of their own professional competence and *both teachers' and parents'* self-esteem ... *emotions often get in the way of constructive planning.'* (my emphasis)
> (Gray & Panter, 2000)

Feelings run high around these children and their at times seemingly inexplicable, unmanageable behaviour. When I run parents' groups in school, the feelings in the room about their children and the school quickly become very obvious. The main emotions which the parents and carers often show and talk about are:

- Anger   at themselves, the child, the school, other family members
- Sadness   for the child, the family, the situation
- Fear   of not being good enough, of their child's negative future prospects
- Isolation   from other parents who might judge them, from the positive aspects of school, from their child and their child's way of thinking
- Blame   of themselves, the child, the school, the authorities, absent partners
- Shame   about their parenting skills, past experiences, inability to understand or connect with school

Using the RETHINK model

These are all very powerful feelings, which can become overwhelming and spill out into interactions with school staff. It's worth remembering how painful such feelings can be when we're meeting with parents/carers; how much they too are having to handle.

In this chapter, I will look at the factors involved in conducting meetings with parents/carers so that these feelings can be recognised and worked with, leading to more positive outcomes for all involved - staff, parents, and most importantly, the child. I will show how we can use the **RETHINK** model and an adaptation of the ten basic principles to give us insight into the behaviour of everyone involved in these meetings, and how to develop strategies for responding to the most challenging comments teachers say they hear most frequently.

Bearing these principles in mind, we can use the **RETHINK** model to structure our thinking around meetings with parents/carers.

PRINCIPLE 1   Behaviour and language can be a form of communication about the parent's anxieties about their children and school, as well as a communication about the parent's own early years and their school experience

PRINCIPLE 2   Parents are doing the best they can with the resources they have. They are not deliberately trying to be difficult. They may be looking for answers too

PRINCIPLE 3   There has to be a two-way partnership between us and the parent. This means we may have to accept and listen to suggestions which we don't agree with

PRINCIPLE 4   It is essential to stay focused on the primary task of learning and how best to help the child. We should not be distracted by our personal views of the parents

PRINCIPLE 5   We cannot change parents/carers, only our reaction to them: but what we do may well create the possibility of them doing things differently

PRINCIPLE 6   Curiosity is core to working with families in challenging situations

PRINCIPLE 7   Non-judgmental descriptions can help us find effective solutions. Blaming doesn't help anyone, but is often our first reaction with parents. Challenging behaviour is an emotive issue for everyone

PRINCIPLE 8   A trial-and-error approach is most productive. There are no easy answers

PRINCIPLE 9   Holding onto the ability to think, and not just react, is crucial

PRINCIPLE 10   We need to notice what is working and do more of it

Preparing for meetings

Before we look at specific examples, it's important to think about how you approach meetings with parents/carers, particularly those you're anticipating will be difficult. Begin by noticing what feelings you have about the meeting. Your feelings may be apparent even before you call a parent/carer to arrange a meeting. For example, do you find yourself saying, *"There's no point in my ringing Mrs A, she never comes into school; she isn't supportive, she doesn't care about her son"* - or something similar?

These are examples of mind-reading and interpretation, and not very helpful. Perhaps Mrs A never comes in because she is only called in for bad news; maybe the times aren't convenient for her; maybe she has other young children; maybe she has problems leaving the house; or perhaps she had an awful time at school herself as a child, and is frightened of a repeat experience of humiliation with an authority figure.

This type of thinking could also be an example of an unconscious defence mechanism such as *projection*, on your own part. You may be projecting your own sense of helplessness or hopelessness about your dealings with the child, into the parent.

Choosing to **review** the situation and **reframe** your own thoughts will enable you to feel some empathy for what you're both dealing with: you'll find it easier to call the parent and to try to arrange something mutually convenient.

Once a meeting has been set up, prepare for it by managing your own emotional state. Notice if you're getting worried or anxious about the meeting. I'm sure we've all felt like this before a meeting with the parents of the kids in this book, at some time or another. We tend to expect the worst and indeed, our past experience may be that our meetings haven't gone well. In addition, colleagues often have their own horror stories about dealing with certain parents/carers. They will say things such as:

> *"Be careful with Mr Y, he can be very aggressive and abusive ..., don't bother with Milly's dad, you'll get nowhere ... he's complained about us in the past ... neither him or his wife are very supportive..."*

These may be versions of the truth, but going into meetings with these kinds of thoughts ringing in our ears is likely to be very counter-productive. Choose to have a more open attitude. Family therapists suggest maintaining a real sense of curiosity about interactions in any meetings with family groups and I've found this a very useful approach to take. If you are *curious* about what will happen and see the meeting as an information-gathering and sharing opportunity, you will be less anxious about how things go. Indeed you will probably find that going into a meeting with an attitude of curiosity and without the need to offer ready-made solutions frees up your thinking, makes you less likely to react defensively, and allows you to really listen to what is happening for the parent/carer and their child.

It is impossible to control all the variables. Remember that the parents are also likely to be dealing with powerful feelings, such as those listed above, and these may show in a variety of ways. The main feeling may initially *appear* to be anger, expressed at the school, the child, the world. However, anger is often a secondary emotion, covering a range of more vulnerable feelings which can include fear, shame, disappointment and inadequacy.

If a parent often misses meetings, try to find a time and a place which is convenient for them. It can be constructive to enlist the help of someone the parent might trust, particularly if you have a Learning Mentor or Home School Support worker in your school. It will be important to find a way to think together about what happens in your meetings with parents/carers, just as it is essential with the 'challenging' pupils in your class.

Just as there is a core range of kids' behaviour which really challenge teachers worldwide, I've found there are a small set of parents' comments and reactions which teachers frequently find difficult, and ask me about in my workshops. So I'm going to address how to work with six typical comments using the **RETHINK** model. I've grouped the **respond** strategies at the end of each section.

Challenging comments

COMMENT I

Parent comment

> *"You say his behaviour is unmanageable in school, but I can't do anything with him at home either!"*

Teacher's internal response

> *"I feel sorry for this parent, but also frustrated - what am I supposed to do if she gives up so easily?"*

STAGE I *REVIEW*

With this type of comment, it can be useful to **review** how the meeting started. Did the teacher start with a long list of the child's misdemeanours and wrongdoings, which led immediately to the parent being overwhelmed by negativity and drawn into feelings of hopelessness? If we start the meeting on a negative note, we can find ourselves stuck with a list of problems rather than solutions. We need to ensure we start meetings in a more positive way, for example, naming a strength which the student has, or, if that is difficult, something we would like them to aspire to. For example:

> *"We all know that Ryan is an intelligent, humorous boy who can be really helpful, particularly with younger pupils. I'd really like to see him fulfil his potential and for us to talk about how we can make sure this happens. I'm concerned, as I am sure you are, because he isn't getting on as well as I would hope he could".*

You can then move on to the specific issues.

STAGE 2   *REFRAME*

We can **reframe** the language we use to talk about what's been happening. As with the kids, it's important to be specific in our description of the problematic behaviour and to relate this to the child's learning needs. For example, *"Ryan doesn't listen in class"* is not describing behaviour, it's giving our judgment of it. Instead, if we use a sentence such as: *"When I'm giving instructions, Ryan looks out of the window and I think he isn't listening and I need him to listen in order to learn"*, it gives both you and Ryan's parent/carer a clear behaviour to discuss. Perhaps he does this at home; perhaps he does it at certain times, after certain triggers: or his mother tells you that he only started staring into space after his grandmother died. This can lead into a far more productive discussion about what is going on for Ryan, and avoids either you or the parent being drawn into an exchange of feelings of hopelessness.

STAGE 3   *REFLECT*

Take a step back and **reflect** on the feelings in the room. In the above example, the teacher is experiencing feelings of futility and frustration, which could be an example of the unconscious defence mechanism of *projection*, telling us something about the feelings of the parent. This might be useful information. You can use this understanding to manage your own state, and if appropriate, name some of the feelings for the parent (*see below*).

Similarly, as the teacher, you might find yourself feeling sorry for the parent/carer and wanting to reassure them, when in fact there are specific issues you need to confront. This could be an example of being caught in a transference of learned helplessness; you are being drawn into almost a parent/child relationship. You need to keep the boundaries as adult-to-adult in order to break this transference and deal with the issues.

STAGE 4 *RESPOND*

Strategies

- ✔ Start the meeting on a positive note by naming some of the student's strengths
- ✔ Build rapport with the parent by focusing on shared positive feelings rather than being drawn into the negative
- ✔ Describe the behaviour separately from your interpretation of it and avoid negative identity-level statements
- ✔ Be aware of projection. If appropriate, name the feeling you are having in a way which includes both of you:

  "It can sometimes feel hard to think about how to manage Ryan's behaviour, perhaps you feel a bit stuck as well ... and I wonder what we can do".

- ✔ Keep the relationship as an adult-adult and do not collude with the helplessness of the parent/carer. Maintain the use of 'we'.

COMMENT 2

Parent comment

"I don't ring you up to ask for help in my work, so why do you ring me about my child when you're supposed to be dealing with him during school hours? It's not my problem if you can't do your job"

Teacher internal response

"This comment really made me angry: what am I supposed to say to that? What a stupid thing to say, and completely irrelevant. I find it really hard to deal with this person when all they do is attack me, and all I'm trying to do is help their child learn. I wonder why I bother"

STAGE 1   *REVIEW*

When a parent reacts with such anger to a call from the school, we can begin by **reviewing** the way this parent is usually contacted by the school. We should **review** how often this parent is telephoned in a day or a week, and by how many people. Perhaps she is getting calls from several people, all complaining about her son. Could one person be appointed to make any calls that are needed, and only after all other avenues have been exhausted? Is the parent only contacted with bad news and if so, can staff try to find some positive reasons to contact home?

STAGE 2   *REFRAME*

The teacher in this example feels attacked and blamed by the parent. Her response is an angry counter-attack. This isn't unusual: it's difficult to remain calm and objective when we're on the receiving end of such harsh feelings. We need to find ways to **reframe** the meaning of the parent's reaction; we can try to find a positive intention in their behaviour. We could choose to believe that the parent is actually showing the teacher that they trust her to do her job without parental interference, and that they don't feel they have anything to add to the situation. If you choose to believe this, you will react more positively to the comment.

We could also **reframe** by choosing to ignore the actual words and empathise with the feelings. The teacher might be the safest person with whom the parent can vent their anger and frustration. As with some of the kids, this behaviour might be showing you that they believe you are strong enough to handle it. If you choose to believe this, you might simply comment on the underlying feelings being expressed. As described above, the main emotion might not be anger: it might be disappointment, hurt or even sadness.

STAGE 3 *REFLECT*

We can take this further and **reflect** some more on the feelings in the communication. This parent may well be feeling attacked and useless and their instinctive 'reptilian brain response' to attack ('fight, flight or freeze' - *see p.104-5*) is to lash out, to fight. They are probably also feeling hurt and ashamed to be called at work or during the day, perhaps seeing this as a sign to everyone that their child is totally unmanageable. This may well be an example of the unconscious mechanism of displacement: the anger the parent is feeling has turned on to the person making the call and may be really meant for themselves, the child or an absent partner.

STAGE 4 *RESPOND*

Strategies

✓ Agree on a whole school approach to contacting this parent, perhaps a certain person who only does this when it's absolutely necessary. Make a set time to call - maybe the end of the week, so that you can give an overall review of the child's behaviour. Make sure good news is also given, so that not every call is talk about the negative

✔ Ask the parent/carer if there are other family members who can be called in an emergency, such as the child needing to be sent home for their own safety. Sometimes a grandparent is more easily available than a working parent

✔ Think about how the meetings have been set up and managed, as this parent/carer seems to be reacting negatively to the school approach. What are the underlying unconscious messages about power? Where does the meeting take place? Is the member of staff behind a big desk and the parent/carer sitting like a child on the other side? Is everyone else sitting down in the room before the parent enters, and is this like being ushered in to see the headteacher and being told off? Make sure the parent/carer is not kept waiting like a naughty child outside the headteacher's office

✔ Hold out your hand to shake theirs when you first meet; this crosses a physical barrier

✔ Be careful about how many staff attend these meetings - too many potentially risks creating a 'ganging up' scenario. Ensure the parent has someone to support them

✔ Be careful about the use of names in a meeting with more than one person. If all the professionals are using first names with each other, does that immediately exclude the parent/carer?

✔ Remember that the feelings might not be meant for you. Tell yourself, *"It's not meant for me"*. At the same time, acknowledge the feelings which might be underlying the parent's anger: *"I can see you are angry/ disappointed/upset/frustrated to be called in again … and I'd like us to find a way to work together on this"*

✔ Practise using language which defuses conflict. For example, use the NLP technique of *'Stack up 'Yes' responses'*. This means you begin the conversation by saying a quick succession of things which you know the parent will agree with. For example: *"Thank you for coming in today, I know you are very busy and had to take time off work; you are obviously very keen to get this sorted out and you want the best for your child, as do we".*

✔ Use inclusive language. For example, replace any '*buts*' with '*and*'. So, instead of saying *"I understand you are angry, but we do need to discuss your son's behaviour"*, say *"I understand you are angry AND we need to discuss your son's behaviour"*. This de-escalates possible conflict as the brain hears both parts of the sentence.

✔ Find a positive intention in the communication, and act accordingly

COMMENT 3

Parent comment

"He's not like that for me at home".

Teacher internal response

"They must be lying, how can that child be so badly behaved at school and then a little angel at home? I don't believe it, or if he is, I bet he is allowed to do exactly what he likes and that's why we can do nothing with him in class".

STAGE 1 REVIEW

You can again begin by **reviewing** how the child's behaviour has been described to the parent/carer. Has it been specifically described, or has vague, judgmental language been used? The teacher may have used statements such as *"He's rude, he never sits still, he doesn't listen"*. All these are interpretations. The parent's response could actually be an honest one: they don't see 'rudeness' at home because their interpretation of 'rude' is the not the same as yours. Describe specifically what and where the relevant incidents have taken place. Think about what it is about the learning task that caused the incident or what the triggers for the behaviour seem to be. Does it always happen, for example, in unstructured free time, in the playground, before a break? State the objective facts simply, in neutral, un-emotive language.

You can also **review** how you are listening to this parent. If you find yourself in strong disagreement, the chances are that you stopped listening at the point where you thought the parent was lying and began, instead, to prepare your own response in your mind. By really listening, focusing on what the parent is really saying, maybe allowing a silence to last slightly beyond your normal limits of comfort, you will hear more from the parent about what is actually happening.

STAGE 2 *REFRAME*

The teacher is framing this parent's reaction as a sign of lying or weak parenting. As in Comment 2 above, you can choose instead to find a positive intention in the parent's response. For example, **reframe** the parent's reaction as genuine bewilderment at the difference in their child's behaviour at home and at school, rather than implied blame about the teacher and the school. Treat the positive intention as the parent wanting to explore the reality of the two situations further, or find out exactly what is different from home and school.

STAGE 3 *REFLECT*

Reflect on the feelings underlying this reaction. This could be an example of the unconscious defence mechanism of denial: rather than bear thinking about an overwhelming feeling, we deny its existence, push it away. It is interesting to notice the similarity between the feelings of the teacher and the parent. The parent is saying there isn't a problem and the teacher, by starting to think that weak parental boundaries are the reason for her own inability to manage the child in class, is also not owning the problem.

This comment - *"He's not like that with me at home"* - could also be an indication of a different set of boundaries and way of communicating at home to school. This might have to be explored. For example, some children are used to being treated more as an equal at home, and can't recognise the power hierarchies that inevitably operate in school. They might also behave differently at home because it's the learning task they need to focus on in school that is challenging for them.

STAGE 4 *RESPOND*

Strategies

- ✔ Describe the behaviour specifically and separate this clearly from your interpretation: *"When Billy says he doesn't see why we have to do an exercise, it's stupid, I think he is being rude"* (the parent might see this as Billy legitimately expressing his opinion)
- ✔ Look for a positive intention in the parent's comments and reactions
- ✔ Notice if you are pushing the problem away from you and being drawn into a 'blame' approach. Focus on the task of discussing the child's learning needs
- ✔ Acknowledge that there might be different rules in different places and that some of the issue is about behaviour which is inappropriate in a larger class setting
- ✔ Discuss the issue, not the feelings. You might have different opinions about parenting, but that isn't the point!
- ✔ Use an exploratory approach to the meeting. See it as an opportunity to share views
- ✔ Use open-ended questions to elicit information, for example *"How?... What?... Tell me?"* rather than *"Why?"*, which often puts people on the defensive

COMMENT 4

Parent comment

> "It's his dad's fault. Whenever he goes to his dad's house, he's spoilt and allowed to do what he likes, and when he comes back home he's completely out of control, demanding and abusive to me"

Teacher internal response

> "No wonder Jack is like he is, there's no consistency: how are we supposed to deal with him if they can't agree?"

STAGE 1 **REVIEW**

There is obviously a potentially tricky situation here with the parents' arrangements for custody of the child. It is important not to get drawn into taking sides - albeit unwittingly. You need to begin by **reviewing** the rules for contacting these parents/carers and check that the correct person is being contacted. If the school always contacts the mother, is this because there is a court order in place or has it been automatically assumed that the father is not involved in the child's schooling? Has the father ever been asked to meetings, and should he be? It would seem important to find out if it's possible for the parents/carers to present a united front.

STAGE 2 **REFRAME**

The mother's response could be **reframed** as showing how anxious she is, and how overwhelmed by her responsibilities she feels, as opposed to wanting to abdicate responsibility. If you **reframe** with a positive intention, you will respond more positively yourself. You can't know, in any case, what the parent's real intention is without exploring further.

STAGE 3 *REFLECT*

This could be an example of the defence of *splitting*, taking up opposing views, seeing things or people as all good or all bad: you are being invited to join in on one side or the other. This can even happen in a meeting with both parents, where they appear to blame each other for what's going on with their child. Again, it's important to work out what's actually happening and how this might be affecting school. Notice if you're being drawn into solidarity for one parent over the other, and take a step back from the situation. It's, however, useful information for you about how the child might be feeling, caught in the middle, and could explain some of their behaviour at school.

STAGE 4 *RESPOND*

Strategies

- ✔ Try to get both parents into school if at all possible, so that there is less chance of splitting and blaming
- ✔ Reflect back the feeling *"That must be very frustrating for you"*, without taking sides.
  "I wonder what helps Jack settle again and how we can use this in school" might be a way of moving this on
- ✔ Give both parents a common positive intention.
  "You obviously love your son and both want the best for him"
- ✔ Reframe the comment as an anxiety and if appropriate, name it

COMMENT 5

Parent comment

"How do you know this was Mark's fault? That teacher doesn't like him anyway, she's always picking on him. I know Liam was also there, and Mrs A didn't say anything to him"

Teacher internal response

"Oh that's handy, blame the teachers, we're always at fault, I'm fed up with it", or,

"I know Mrs A was talking about Mark in the staffroom as if she really does hate him, what am I supposed to say? It might be unfair"

STAGE 1 *REVIEW*

This can be a very difficult situation, particularly if you have some sympathy for the parent/carer's point of view. Be prepared to **review,** and do a survey of all the child's classes to find out where the problems are actually arising for this pupil - is it only with certain teachers, times or subjects? Issues do arise between particular teachers and pupils, as we are all only human. On the other hand, it might be that the pupil is struggling with a particular *subject*, and is voicing this as a dislike of the teacher. This often happens when pupils feel they aren't coping in a class: the pupil sees it as a relationship matter between them and the teacher.

If a parent/carer is being continually contacted by one department, there is obviously an issue which needs to be resolved, and it might not be a whole school issue.

STAGE 2 *REFRAME*

We can begin again by **reframing** the context and deflecting away from the personal by focusing on the specific behaviours which are causing concern. **Reframe** this potentially challenging statement as offering the school an opportunity to find out exactly what is going wrong for the child.

You need to keep to specifics and describe the inappropriate behaviour without interpretation. It can be difficult if you want to support your colleague and don't want to appear to be taking sides in the argument. You can comment on the parent/carer's feelings, without having to agree with their attack.

STAGE 3 *REFLECT*

This parent's reaction to a certain member of staff and desire to blame him for her son's problems could be an example of *transference*. The parent is experiencing school and school staff in the same way that they did when they were pupils themselves. This can be triggered for some parents very early in their visit - by, for example, the smell when they walk into the school, the sign on the door, the gates... These parents need to be encouraged to separate out their own experience from that of their child, and you need to avoid being drawn into being whatever kind of teacher they used to have - advising, lecturing, punitive.

It can also be useful to reflect on what is happening in the room between the parent and the child. If the child is there with the parent/carer, notice in particular any parental actions which are mirrored by the child's behaviour. In cases such as the one described above, the child can sometime be very blaming towards the mother as well: it would then seem that the mother needs to displace this feeling somewhere else, as she can't withstand the onslaught. You will often see learned responses and behaviours which are then re-enacted in your classroom.

STAGE 4 *RESPOND*

Strategies

✔ You can acknowledge the feeling without being distracted from your task of addressing the child's behaviour and learning:

"I know you are a great support to your son and you don't want him to be blamed unfairly, neither do we. That's why we have tried to find out all the facts".

✔ Acknowledge any objections without necessarily agreeing with them:

"I understand that you think this isn't fair and you feel angry on Mark's behalf, and we do need to sort this out in the best way for him and everyone else"

✔ If you feel you have to support colleagues but are unsure about what happened, you can simply say,

"I wasn't there, I can't comment on that. What I would like to do is make sure this kind of problem doesn't happen again … what's the best way forward?"

✔ Notice the interaction between parent and child and how this relates to the relationship observed between child and teachers.

COMMENT 6

Parent comment

"I want him taken away, I'm sick of him, I've told the Social Worker and I've told him that he will be put away, he's affecting all my other children and ruining our family'

Teacher internal response

"Oh my god, what am I supposed to do now, I'm not a Social Worker, she should be here to sort this out"

STAGE 1 REVIEW

This comment would appear to suggest that other professionals are involved with this family and you might not have been aware of this. **Review** what you know about who else is involved with this child. Find out what other meetings are taking place. This issue may well be for discussion in another inter-agency meeting, which you may have input into without having to attend.

In relation to this particular meeting, you can **review** how you started the meeting and what was said at the beginning. Perhaps you started by saying something negative about the pupil's relationships with other children? This might have triggered the parent's response about other children in the family. **Review** if the child needs to attend meetings if you know the parent/carer has the potential to be very blaming. It might be better to meet the parent separately first. **Review** if there any adults who can attend the meeting to support the child, someone who works positively with him and can add some balance to the comments.

An example of a conversation with parents

Teacher   "Thank you for coming in here today. I know you want to get this sorted out as much as we do and you obviously care about your daughter, Shanice. I can understand you are upset, and that's why I thought we needed to meet face to face so that we can work together on this"

Parent 1   "I am sick of this school calling me up here to talk about her behaviour. I don't ring the school when she misbehaves at home, why should they ring me when they can't deal with her?"

Teacher   "I understand that must be annoying sometimes. It's just that we would rather work together with you on this. We could have just sent her home, but I would rather find a way to deal with this so it doesn't happen again. We do appreciate your continuing support, even thought it's frustrating. What do you find works at home with Shanice?"

Parent 1   "Well, she goes to work with her uncle Dave on Saturday and she is good as gold. Dave always says he wasn't much good at school and not doing well there never did him any harm"

Teacher   "Well, that's interesting, I wonder if Shanice perhaps feels more confident and relaxed with her uncle, maybe the more practical side of things and being outside suits her. So I guess we need to find a way to get her to feel more confident about school and perhaps she can help out in the same way here sometimes, and then in year 10, we can look at work experience. Of course, as you know, the reality at the moment is that there are not many apprenticeships around nowadays and a lot of competition for them. So Shanice does need to stay in school until at least 16 and get the best she can from it".

Parent 2 "Well, she is just like me. I hated school"

Teacher "And that's very honest of you to admit that, thanks. Hopefully schools have changed a bit since then, and I do think that there are things in school which Shanice actually likes and she can do. I've noticed she is very good at woodwork and graphic design. She just seems to lack motivation sometimes".

Parent 2 "Yes, well, school's boring, innit?"

Parent 1 "Shut up, John, you're not helping. The thing is, to be honest, we can't do anything with her at home either. She just does what she wants".

→ **Notice here the two reactions. This is what Parent 1 is experiencing. Think about what the feeling and underlying issues might be.**

Teacher "It can be really hard knowing what to do with Shanice, especially when she doesn't want to do something, that's what I mean about motivation and I agree, like everything, some parts of school can be boring for all of us! I wonder what does motivate her. As I said, I've noticed she really loves woodwork and is really good at it".

Parent 2 "Is she? She never tells us"

Teacher "Well, yes, it can be hard to know what teenagers are thinking sometimes. Shall we see if we can make a plan on how to build on her strengths and motivate her a bit better with other things? How about we agree to let you know at the end of the week how things have been going, and make sure we include some positive things, so it's not all bad news for you. Also, maybe we could think about how to use Shanice's skills to help out a bit in the school in general and set some targets with her. I could also get her to have a chat with the careers person about future jobs and training so she knows what she needs to do".

STAGE 2 **REFRAME**

You can **reframe** this interaction as giving you very important information about how overwhelmed the parent is feeling. It also gives you clear information about messages the child is getting. It would be very important to retain some positive focus in your dealings with the parent, and especially with the child.

STAGE 3 **REFLECT**

We can **reflect** on the feelings which seem to be underlying the comments. There is a kind of hopelessness and powerlessness in this statement. The child is being allowed to become omnipotent - someone that no-one can control and who affects everyone else in the family. By association, the parent is perhaps feeling that she is a 'bad' parent, without any power to act appropriately. Perhaps she has not had an early experience of having her own feelings 'contained' and managed.

STAGE 4 **RESPOND**

Strategies

- ✔ Check if a Social Worker is already involved: put the parent in touch with anyone in your school who offers family support and liaision. Be careful not to make the whole meeting about this: you need to stick to issues in school. Keep the emphasis on the child's learning and the primary aim of your meeting

- ✔ **Reframe** the meeting as an opportunity to find out and share information rather than just to draw up a solution. Keep careful notes which you can pass on for input into any other meetings around the child

✔ Make sure you have informed your designated child protection person about the issues arising in the meeting. You do not have to deal with all of this yourself

✔ Remember the actual words and threats could just be an indication of the parent's overwhelming feelings. If appropriate, name the parental anxiety. For example, *"It must be very hard not to feel bad when your child seems out of control and you really want to help him"*

✔ Notice if this child is becoming omnipotent around the school. Is this the child no-one can deal with positively? What has happened to all the adults in this relationship? Make sure you have some concrete plans and strategies for dealing with the behaviour

✔ Focus on any positives about the child

✔ Avoid being drawn into splitting, with another agency as the enemy. You might have displaced feelings about not being able to help the family and these feelings can lead you to want to blame another agency for not solving the problem. You need to be aware when this happening for you - this is your own issue, and should not interfere with how you conduct the school meeting

Conclusion

Preparation for meetings with parents/carers is vital, just as it is for teaching. It's important to be clear about the outcome you are hoping for from the meeting: this might be simply to gain more information about what's going on for the child. Have some strategies prepared to create a positive start, and then to defuse any potential conflicts if necessary. However, be equally aware of what you can't control. You won't change the family dynamic or 'make' the parents change their parenting in a meeting. You can retain your own sense of the child.

Whatever happens is information, as it gives a clear indication of some of the interactions and issues at home. It may be that this, at the very least, will help you understand the child's behaviour in your class.

You'll know when a parent who was challenging is becoming easier to work with when ...

★ you don't put off making that call to her

★ she answers the phone to you!

★ you are not continually looking at the clock in meetings with her

★ she offers to help you with something

★ you can have a bit of normal 'chit-chat' or even some humour in a meeting with her

★ she asks to see you when there's a problem

Chapter 10

"What can I do with the colleague who…?"

Working with challenges from colleagues

In my workshops and trainings, I meet many teachers who like the ideas presented in this book and who want to share their new thinking with colleagues back at school. However, many of these participants say they almost dread having to explain the ideas to some of their colleagues who appear resistant and even dismissive of this way of thinking. Meg, a teacher in secondary, explains it as follows:

> "I really like the idea of using frameworks and therapeutic ideas to think about behaviour, and I believe it's vital for us to know how early childhood trauma affects pupils' learning. I also know that I need to develop my self-awareness and self-reflection. But many of my colleagues don't see the point. They think it's all a bit 'pink and fluffy' and a waste of time. They just want to deal with the behaviour in an action-and-consequence kind of way, and I really don't know how to persuade them otherwise. I find it totally frustrating; sometimes I even feel like giving up".

As with parents/carers, it can be useful to use the **RETHINK** approach to think about our dealings with colleagues. Remember that challenging behaviour can make us all feel incompetent and de-skilled, and this sense of powerlessness, of not immediately knowing *the* answer, will lead some staff to react defensively and even aggressively to new suggestions for strategies. It can be dispiriting to try very hard to understand a child's behaviour, and then to have the sense that the action or inaction of a colleague is undermining our efforts. If we're not careful, this can lead us into feeling negative about working with that colleague, or even to giving up with the child, rather than confront the issue with another member of staff.

The kind of comments we hear from colleagues which are the most disheartening and frustrating can generally be divided into three groups:

Objections to the implied role of the teacher or model of teaching

"I'm a teacher, not a therapist or a social worker"

"It's a load of mumbo jumbo, not practical at all"

"You are too soft with those kids"

Objections related to time and environment

"It takes too long to think like this"

"That's OK for 1-2-1, but you can't do it in a class"

"I'm not trained to do this, and I don't have time to spend on it"

Objections to giving misbehaving children more attention

"What about the good kids in the class?"

"I have to teach for exams and these kids interfere with what I'm trying to do"

"I don't know why you bother with him, he even turns on you when he's angry"

So we need to find common ground and a way forward with colleagues who make comments like these. To do this, we can look at what's happening between us by adapting the ten principles for dealing with pupils' challenging behaviour, just as we did in the last chapter for our work with parents and carers.

PRINCIPLE 1   Behaviour and language can be a form of communication about our colleague's anxieties concerning their capabilities, and the pressures they may be facing

PRINCIPLE 2   Colleagues are doing the best they can with the resources they have. They are not deliberately trying to be difficult. When they don't know or aren't sure, they are likely to revert to extreme patterns of behaviour and look to the school policy as a way of asserting clear boundaries

PRINCIPLE 3   There has to be a two-way partnership between us and our colleagues. This means we may have to accept and listen to suggestions which we don't agree with ourselves

PRINCIPLE 4   It is essential to stay focused on the primary task of learning and how best to help the child. We should not be distracted by our personal views of the child, his or her parents/carers, or our colleagues

PRINCIPLE 5   We cannot change our colleagues, only our reaction to them: but what we do may well create the possibility of them doing things differently

PRINCIPLE 6   Curiosity is core to working with colleagues' 'challenging behaviour'. Whatever you notice happening is useful information

PRINCIPLE 7   Non-judgmental descriptions can help us find effective solutions. Blaming doesn't help anyone, and is often our first reaction with colleagues who seem to have different philosophies. Children's challenging behaviour is an emotive issue for everyone

PRINCIPLE 8   A trial-and-error approach is most productive. There are no easy answers and no 'one size fits all' solutions

PRINCIPLE 9   Holding onto the ability to think, and not just react, is crucial

PRINCIPLE 10   We need to notice what is working, do more of it, and support our colleagues in doing more of what they find works

Bearing these principles in mind should help us to work better with our colleagues as much as with the pupils. Let's now look at three statements which encompass the more common criticisms levelled at this way of working, and use the **RETHINK** model to address them. As in the previous chapter, I'll be grouping the strategies into the **Respond** section after the three earlier stages of **Review, Reframe** and **Reflect**.

COMMENT I

"I'm a teacher, not a therapist or a social worker"

STAGE I *REVIEW*

We could **review** what is happening to trigger this remark. Has this colleague been teaching a lot of classes with challenging children from troubled backgrounds? Does the teacher feel supported by colleagues in their dealing with this type of student? Is there a plan in place across lessons with practical strategies which all teachers feel they can use? Sometimes a colleague makes a remark like this when he or she feels overwhelmed by the problems they are experiencing in their own classes.

We can also **review** the conversation or incident which led up to this remark which can often be triggered by a certain type of word or suggestion. For example, if a teacher is feeling particularly stressed and tired, and the conversation started with comments about how stressful the child's life is at the moment, the teacher may react angrily; they may feel that their own feelings are being ignored or left unacknowledged. You can check out this possibility by naming any underlying feelings you feel your colleague might be showing. You might say, for example:

"I think it can sometimes feel as if we're being asked to solve all the world's problems, and that can be really worrying and upsetting"

When **reviewing** how this conversation started, we can also think back to whether the first comments focused on the child's family problems and emotional difficulties, or whether there was any focus on the link with learning. When the link with teaching and learning isn't made explicit, and new strategies are suggested which seem outside a specifically educational frame of reference, teachers may react in a seemingly dismissive way: this can be particularly the case if the suggestions appear to come from someone who isn't a classroom teacher, such as a counsellor or mentor. It's very important, therefore, to make it clear that the need to think differently is related to *improving a child's capacity to benefit from teaching*.

STAGE 2 *REFRAME*

We may need to **reframe** our own reaction to the comment *"I'm a teacher, not a therapist or a social worker"*. It can be hard not to react defensively and angrily on hearing this, particularly if we feel very strongly that we know the best way to help a child. We could **reframe** the information in the comment as telling us something about our colleagues's feelings, rather than as an example of his or her resistance to suggestions. We can do this, as we did with the pupils and parents/carers, by separating out our colleague's behaviour/words and our interpretation of it. For example:

DESCRIPTION	INTERPRETATIONS AND FEELINGS
"When my colleague says he is not
a counsellor or social worker,	*... I **interpret** that as meaning he isn't interested in my way of working"*

Obviously, separating this out for ourselves will show us that these two thoughts are not necessarily connected as directly as we had previously thought. We could choose to interpret the comment as meaning that the teacher doesn't think he or she has the necessary skills for this situation, and that perhaps we do. By **reframing** with a positive intention, we will manage our own reaction far more appropriately.

From another perspective, we could **reframe** the comment as a strong identity level statement. What does being a teacher mean to this colleague, and why do they feel so attacked by our ideas? Again, perhaps it's a sign of feeling unskilled and out of their comfort zone. If we identify a skills gap, we may be able to help with support and training.

STAGE 3 *REFLECT*

We can also **reflect** on the underlying anxieties behind such a strongly expressed statement. Maybe this teacher is feeling very unsure about what to do. If we find ourselves becoming very angry or feeling hopeless in the exchange, it could be an example of *projection*, giving us information about how our colleague could be feeling. Or it could be an example of *displacement*, and, as with the kids, it may help us to think: *"This is not meant for me"*, or *"Who or what is my colleague actually angry about?"*

STAGE 4 *RESPOND*

Strategies

✔ Acknowledge your colleague's objections and feelings

   "I know, we're not social workers, and sometimes it feels as if we're being asked to do everything. That can feel really overwhelming and frustrating"

✔ Encourage the colleague to avoid focusing on a separation between the job roles of a teacher and, for example, a social worker, by acknowledging the objection and taking the conversation forward to teaching solutions. It shouldn't be an *'either ... or'* situation, so use the word *'and'* in your follow-on remarks

"…and at the same time we know that trauma and worries from home do have an effect on pupils' learning"

✔ Make the actual effects of trauma on learning clear

"…so that might explain why Jez can't concentrate, his mind is so full up with other things"

✔ Make it clear that these are not 'miraculous' solutions, and that the teacher isn't expected to solve all the child's problems

✔ "What I'm suggesting is just another way of finding strategies which might work: we both know nothing is foolproof. Perhaps it's worth giving it a go to see what happens"

✔ Use your own experience and empathise with their position

"I feel like that too, and this actually helped me feel better, I found it useful"

✔ Use inclusive 'we' to show your solidarity in thinking as a teacher

✔ If a colleague is reacting defensively and feeling blamed, affirm their strengths wherever possible:

"I understand what you're saying: I did notice however that Anthony responds well to your style of teaching, perhaps you're showing you understand his situation by giving him the boundaries he needs'

✔ Be aware of the possibility of projection and displacement. Use this as information to reframe your own reactions

COMMENT 2

It takes too long to think like this, I don't have the time

STAGE 1 *REVIEW*

The issue of lack of time is often raised as an objection to thinking about pupils in a different way. We should remember, however, that we always seem to find time for the things we believe are important. When a colleague offers this objection, we can begin by **reviewing** with them how much time is already spent in meetings, 'phone calls and discussions about the particularly challenging pupil. This colleague might already have spent a lot of time on this pupil, and felt it was time wasted. We can acknowledge this and suggest that taking a bit of time to think differently might save time in the longer term. At worst, doing something different will bring the same kind of results as the colleague is having at the moment: at best, it will create time.

We might **review** why this teacher is feeling that time is such a scarce resource. Is this a colleague who is having problems with time management in general, or a colleague who agrees to help with all kinds of initiatives and has actually too much to do? If a teacher is feeling overwhelmed by their workload, the idea of giving time to thinking about challenging pupils can be the final straw which tips them over the edge. You might need to support this colleague in reassessing their workload or simply name the issue for them. For example, you might say,

> *"There seems to be far too much to do at the moment, and maybe this makes it seem impossible to spend more time thinking about these kids unless it will save us time in the long-run"*

We can **review** the number of new programmes and initiatives running in the school at the moment. Are your suggestions for rethinking around challenging pupils being put forward in the midst of a lot of pressure to implement other initiatives? If this is the case, you need to link your ideas with any complementary programmes. For example, in secondary schools, the Assessment for Learning Framework and the Coaching Strategy Programme rely on reflection and self-assessment skills, both of which can be linked into training or discussions around the ideas in this book.

We can **review** how meetings about challenging pupils are organised. It could be that the meetings are very reactive and ad-hoc and called by several different people, which might mean a teacher is continually writing reports or giving opinions on particular pupils. It's worth trying to find a way to timetable a regular forum for discussing these children or young people, rather than calling meetings as incidents arise. Perhaps this is something you and your colleague can suggest, and explain why it is necessary. This would involve working together, rather than against each other.

STAGE 2 REFRAME

We can **reframe** for our colleagues the issue of how much time is needed to implement this kind of thinking. We can reassure them that they don't need to go away and train to be therapists, or even read huge number of case notes in pupils' files. The thinking doesn't have to take long. Draw attention to the fact that it doesn't take long to show a pupil you've remembered something about them, and that this small thing might have a huge effect on certain children.

We can **reframe** for ourselves the time it takes to implement this type of thinking in our schools. Small steps can lead to change: it doesn't always require a whole school initiative (although this is obviously helpful). A **reframing** comment can be made in a moment in a corridor when you're talking to a colleague about a child. For example, if the colleague is talking about the pupil's 'bad' behaviour and lack of respect, you can **reframe** what the child is doing as anxiety-driven by saying something as simple as,

"I know that behaviour is really inappropriate, I wonder what he's so anxious about in the learning situation?"

The comments about time could also be **reframed** as showing a training need. If a teacher feels that it's going to take a long time to understand something new, particularly if this new thinking has not been prioritised in the school, it can be difficult to make any time to take the first step. In a busy school year, there are many competing demands on teachers' time and planning.

So perhaps we can **reframe** the new skills in the **RETHINK** model which appear to our colleague to need a lot of time to learn as the difference between *unconscious competence* - when we're very good at something but don't realise how we are doing it - and *conscious competence* - where we know we're good at something and *are* aware of how we're doing it. Then we can look together at what we do that works, skills that perhaps we don't even realise we have, and do more of these, rather than taking lots of time to retrain. For example, most teachers are very good at getting into rapport on good days with pupils; if they become more aware of how they do this, they can do it more often with those they find challenging. This model of looking for strengths will seem less time-consuming than a model which seems to require completely new ways of doing things.

We can also **reframe** the issue of time to that of thinking time. It might be that our colleague is someone who gives him or herself very little time to reflect and think. By simply taking the time to talk to our colleague in a certain way, using reflective listening skills to show empathy, name their feelings and anxieties, you may be helping to create that thinking time and space in their heads so that they can then be freed up to think about the pupils. Finally, assume your colleague has a positive intention in their behaviour and their remarks. Even if they don't, if you assume a negative intention, you will react negatively. For example, you could assume that this colleague wants to take time to really understand your new way of thinking, rather than assuming they don't want to learn something new. You might say,

> *"I know you plan really meticulously, you would want to do this really properly; it could just mean a small shift in thinking, building on what you already do, rather than a whole new subject area which takes ages to learn"*

Similarly it might be an example of a skills gap, where the teacher feels they don't know how to implement this thinking. They will need concrete examples and strategies.

STAGE 3 *REFLECT*

It might be helpful to **reflect** on what might be going on unconsciously in our interactions with our colleagues. When a colleague insists they don't have time for this way of working, it could be an example of the unconscious defence mechanism of *denial*. It might be that they find it too painful to stop and take the time to think about these pupils and their overwhelming needs. Not making time can be a way to protect against thinking unbearable thoughts. It might be useful for us to remember the potential for distress when dealing with this kind of comment.

It might also be an example of *displacement*, where a teacher feels no-one has time to think about them, so they displace this 'lack of time' into their reactions to certain pupils. No-one is 'holding them in mind', so they are unable to hold these pupils in mind. Again, taking time to listen and talk to these colleagues may free up time for them to think about the pupils.

STAGE 4 *RESPOND*

Strategies

✔ Above all, give this colleague time to talk and really listen to their concerns

✔ Name their anxiety about time and being held in mind

   "Sometimes it feels like no-one has time to help or listen to us teachers"

✔ Encourage your colleague to see this model as a time-saver

   "I don't think this way of working should take up a lot of time, we want to save time, not make work for ourselves"

✔ Emphasise that this model builds on what works and what your colleague does well already, thus enhancing good practice rather than replacing it

✔ Give short, simple strategies which do not take a lot of time to learn. For example: *"Some pupils just need feedback on the task, so we can say "That's great", rather than "I think that's great"*

✔ Ask questions where the language quickly focuses on the main issues. For example:*"Maybe we can just take a moment and think about what this behaviour is showing us about Ann's needs or what she hasn't learnt to do yet"*

✔ Be specific in what you notice and give feedback on the learning point *"You really helped Gill the other day when you realised how anxious she was about writing something autobiographical and when you gave her a safe framework to do it"*

✔ Remarks about lack of time are often accompanied by the comment, *"Well, it might be OK for 1-2-1 situations but you can't do it with a class of 30"*. It's therefore essential to focus on giving colleagues easy, do-able strategies rather than complex explanations of the theory

✔ Find a positive intention in your colleague's behaviour and name it

✔ Be aware of any unconscious defence mechanisms in operation and take some time to reflect for yourself on what they might be telling you

✔ Link the new ways of working you want to introduce to other initiatives in the school

✔ Take every opportunity to feed in the kind of language which acknowledges the child's needs and anxieties. Use this language where appropriate to name your colleagues' anxieties as well

COMMENT 3

> "I need to get on with teaching for the exam results and the
> good kids need my attention"

or

> "Other kids are complaining about certain kids getting more attention"

STAGE 1 *REVIEW*

When a teacher constantly makes comments about the need to get good results, we can **review** where this pressure might be coming from. Is it coming from the individual teacher, the head of department, the senior management? How do pupils in this teachers' class do at the moment in exams? It could be an example of a teacher who has always had high achieving classes, or the opposite, a teacher who is being challenged to improve results. Alongside this, we need to **review** the support and help this teacher is getting in relation to their classes. Sometimes a remark like this can highlight a teacher who is struggling with the exam syllabus or who isn't sure exactly what is expected. It can also reflect a changing school culture where a teacher may feels the goalposts have moved. Perhaps this was once a school where exam results were the main focus, and now the teachers are expected to deal successfully with a range of abilities. This is about dealing with change.

We can also **review** how much time we are giving challenging pupils, and how we are in fact rewarding the other pupils. Maybe this teacher is right, and too much time is given to the 'difficult' kids, and the school isn't rewarding appropriate behaviour and learning. Again, this is unlikely to be an *'either ... or'* situation, but it does need to be looked at.

STAGE 2 *REFRAME*

We may need to **reframe** this remark by separating out the behaviour and the interpretation. What is actually happening in the class with this teacher and the pupils, and how is it being interpreted? For example, perhaps other pupils are complaining, but they may not really be that bothered. Kids generally know who needs extra help; the teacher may be displacing his or her own feelings onto these pupils. The **reframe** might be: *"When I spend a lot of time trying to help Angela who is misbehaving, I feel that I'm not being good enough for the quieter kids"*. This is the teacher's issue, not the pupils.

We might need to ask this colleague a question to encourage this separation, for example: *"What are the other pupils doing or saying specifically which makes you think that?"*

Reframe the comments by keeping your own focus on the primary issue: what is the teacher really worried about? As with our dealings with pupils, there will be secondary behaviours displayed by colleagues. The comment about 'other pupils' is a secondary behaviour which should not distract us from discussing the main issues. What other pupils are saying may be largely irrelevant in this context: the issue is why the teacher is being so affected by their attempts to get under her skin.

STAGE 3 *REFLECT*

This remark may be an example of the unconscious defence mechanism of *splitting*. This teacher is becoming polarised in his or her thinking about pupils: they are either all good or all bad. In fact, this might be an example of a *projection* which initially came from the pupil, and which the teacher is picking up on. Children and young people like the ones described in this book often view themselves in an extremely polarised way, as 'bad' and undeserving of positive attention.

We can take a moment to **reflect** on any themes which come up in our discussion with this colleague. If there is a common theme about the unfairness of rewarding 'bad' behaviour or of 'good' behaviour not being noticed, this could be information about the adult's earlier experiences. In a workshop focusing on this issue, James, a deputy headteacher said:

> *"This makes me think of a teacher in my school who continually and aggressively disrupted a recent presentation by a colleague on the new rewards system we intended introducing in our school. I was surprised at the time, since this teacher was quite friendly with the colleague who was presenting the topic. Now I realise that she always interrupts or objects in some way when the word 'praise' or 'reward' is mentioned. I wonder what her early experience of being rewarded or not rewarded was".*

In her reaction to her friend and colleague's presentation, this teacher was perhaps unconsciously re-enacting her own relationship with a parent who was overly critical, or perhaps a sibling who always got praised more than her.

Finally, we could also **reflect** on any feelings which may underlie the statement. The emphasis on *"**I** need to get the exam results"* gives a sense of isolation, and suggests that this teacher might need to be included more in a team, in a shared thinking framework. We need, therefore, to resist the urge to reject further interaction and discussion with her. We need to focus again on that shared goal of improving learning for all.

STAGE 4 *RESPOND*

Strategies

Strategies need to focus on reducing splitting and encouraging teamwork to achieve common goals.

- ✔ Acknowledge if there is a need to reward appropriate behaviour and learning, and at the same time make it clear that these this is not mutually exclusive to thinking about the needs of the more challenging pupils

- ✔ Notice if you are being drawn into a polarised position, where you are always advocating 'for' a particular pupil and a colleague is always 'against'. To resist this unconscious pull, you could, for example, make the distinction between listening to a pupil and condoning their behaviour
  "Listening to this pupil doesn't necessarily mean I agree with what she's saying"

- ✔ Use the technique described in Chapter 8 of 'Stacking up 'yes' responses' to ensure discussion starts on common ground: for example,
  "We all want to get the best from our pupils and to make sure learning can take place: we know some pupils find it difficult to concentrate and it can be very tiring trying to keep them focused, and we need to measure their progress as well"

- ✔ Avoid being distracted into discussions about what other pupils in the class think. Be prepared to challenge the view that other pupils do not want challenging pupils to get help.
  "I understand how difficult it is when other pupils complain, and I think they actually know who needs extra help and why"

- ✔ If other comments are made such as *"He even turns on you"*, treat these as secondary behaviours as well and focus on the issue at hand

- ✔ Offer to work with this colleague on making sure the reward system in the school acknowledges everyone; better still, ask for their help, as you will be modelling the fact that asking for help is not a sign of weakness

✔ Ask open-ended questions to elicit what is really happening for this colleague. Use words such as *"How?"* ... *"What?"* ... and *"Tell me?"*, rather than *"Why?"*, which could elicit a defensive response and won't break the pattern of splitting around these kids

✔ Emphasis that you don't need to be 'strong' and perfect all the time. We all get it wrong with these kids, but we can learn from the mistakes and show them how to repair relationships

You'll know you're making progress with a challenging colleague when ...

★ *you notice that you have a common language which involves discussing a misbehaving pupil's needs and anxieties, not just their behaviour*

★ *your colleague sometimes asks your opinion*

★ *they share a strategy with you which they found works with the pupil*

★ *you hear them mentioning feelings to another member of staff!*

★ *you can disagree honestly about what's best for the pupil without it becoming personal and upsetting; or even have a laugh about it!*

Appendix A

CHECKLIST - USING THE RETHINK MODEL

This checklist is an aide-memoire to help you to think about children in your class whom you find challenging in some way. The questions are designed to guide your thinking around the child and your use of the **RETHINK** model. You may want to photocopy the next four pages so that they are easily accessible when you're tearing your hair out about a particular child!

The more you use the checklist and apply the **RETHINK** model, the more it will become second nature to *Review/Respond, Reframe/Respond, Reflect/Respond.*

Good luck in developing your own resources and strategies with THAT kid!

CHECKLIST - USING THE **RETHINK** MODEL Marie Delaney ISBN 9781903269145 © Worth Publishing

WHAT CAN I DO WITH THE KID WHO …?

STAGE I *REVIEW*

Classroom rules

Are there clear classroom rules, rewards and sanctions?	☐
Is the student clear about them?	☐
How do you know?	
Are they constantly reinforced and checked?	☐

Seating arrangements

Is there a seating plan?	☐
How does this affect this student?	
Can the student hear and see the teacher ?	☐
Is the student sitting with positive peer role models?	☐

Instructions

How are instructions given and checked?	
Are they given verbally, demonstrated and shown visually?	☐
Is an example given by the teacher and then one got from the student?	☐

Learning style

What is this student's preferred learning style?	
Is work presented in a variety of different ways?	☐
Are there visual, auditory and kinaesthetic tasks in the lesson?	☐

Behaviour management

Is there a behaviour plan with clear targets? Was the pupil involved in this?	☐ ☐
How is it monitored?	
Who monitors it?	
Is the inappropriate behaviour in all lessons?	☐
Are there certain triggers - subjects, groupings, time of day?	☐ ☐ ☐
How is inappropriate behaviour dealt with at the moment?	
How is appropriate behaviour dealt with? Is it noticed and acknowledged?	
What is the current pattern of interaction between teacher and student?	

CHECKLIST - USING THE **RETHINK** MODEL Marie Delaney ISBN 9781903269145 © Worth Publishing

FRAMEWORK 1 Where do the feelings come from?

What feelings does the behaviour evoke in you, the teacher?

Where do these feelings come from?

What are the feelings showing about underlying anxieties, expectations and beliefs?

What words are used in the staffroom around this student?

What unconscious defence mechanisms appear to be in operation?

For example, projection, transference, splitting, denial, omnipotence, displacement?

Are there polarised views in the staffroom? Is this an example of splitting?   ☐ ☐

FRAMEWORK 2 Effects of trauma on learning

Is the behaviour showing possible effects of trauma on learning?

For example, following violence, loss, addiction, parental mental illness?   ☐

FRAMEWORK 3 Attachment Patterns and the Learning Triangle

Is the student able to engage in a relationship with the teacher?   ☐

Is the student able to do the task?   ☐

What kind of task engages the student?

How do they approach the task - individually/in group/ with or without adult?

Do they start immediately?   ☐

Do they want to do the task independently or do they need a lot of help?   ☐ ☐

What do they do when they are stuck?   ☐

Can they ask for help?   ☐

Can they wait for help?   ☐

Do they finish the task?   ☐

How important is it to get your attention and involvement?

What is their reaction to praise? *Verbal praise? Written praise?*

What is their reaction to criticism?

What type of attachment pattern might they be exhibiting?

CHECKLIST - USING THE **RETHINK** MODEL Marie Delaney ISBN 9781903269145 © Worth Publishing

FRAMEWORK 4 Play Development

What stage of play is the student at?	
Can they - play alone? ☐ Play alongside? ☐ Play by their own rules? ☐	
Invite others into their play? ☐ Play by others' rules? ☐ Negotiate? ☐	
Take turns? ☐ Lose gracefully? ☐	
What happens when the student loses?	
Does the student accept this?	☐
Does the student cheat or make up new rules if they are losing?	☐
Can the student share and show empathy?	☐

STAGE 2 *REFRAME*

Separating descriptions of behaviour from interpretations

What does the student do SPECIFICALLY which is inappropriate?	
When do they do this? With whom?	
Is it affected by the time of day? By different lessons?	☐ ☐
When do they NOT do it? What is the difference between the situations in which they do and don't display the behaviour?	

Reframing what the behaviour means

How is the teacher interpreting the behaviour?	
Are there examples of negative, judgmental identity statements?	☐
What is the student *actually* doing?	
How could this be interpreted differently?	
What could be a positive intention behind the inappropriate behaviour?	
Is this a learning opportunity?	☐
What skill is the student showing that they have not learnt?	

Reframing feelings

What is the teacher feeling?
What is the student feeling?
What information is this giving about the interaction?

CHECKLIST - USING THE **RETHINK** MODEL Marie Delaney ISBN 9781903269145 © Worth Publishing

STAGE 3 *REFLECT*

What appear to be the student's needs?
Learning needs

Do they lack some of the skills of a good learner?	☐
Do they appear able or unable to…	
- feel safe in learning new skills and be willing to take risks?	☐
- have good self-esteem?	☐
- seek help?	☐
- concentrate and ignore distractions?	☐
- manage frustration, anxiety and disappointment?	☐
- bear not knowing something?	☐
- be optimistic?	☐
- wait for attention?	☐

Unmet needs from earlier experiences

What is the student trying to get or fulfill with this behaviour?
For example, *control, affirmation, lessening of anxiety, safety, power?*

What has the student *not* had experience of?	
- A consistent adult?	☐
- Positive feedback on getting things wrong?	☐
- Containment and naming of overwhelming feelings?	☐

What does it seem that the student *cannot believe*
about the teacher and the classroom?

CHECKLIST - USING THE **RETHINK** MODEL Marie Delaney ISBN 9781903269145 © Worth Publishing

Appendix B

THE IMPORTANCE OF MANAGING OUR OWN STATE

As staff in schools, we manage relationships and deal with a myriad of complex emotions every day. In other professions where this happens, such as Social Care and counselling, time is set aside for staff to discuss their cases with a supervisor, and to process their feelings about the work.

We need to learn from that model, and make time to be consciously more aware of our own physical and emotional states and reflect on our practice. We can then focus on strategies for maintaining a resourceful state for teaching.

How can we manage our state?

1   CREATE POSITIVE ANCHORS

Take some time to create and practise being able to recall a positive anchor, something which will trigger a resourceful feeling in you. For example, one teacher keeps a photo of his wedding on a beach on his desk, but the photo is turned upside down - a visual reminder of a happy event, and a trigger for him to remember to think differently when stuck in a negative interaction with a pupil. An auditory anchor might be the sound of your child laughing, or a favourite song to sing to yourself. A kinaesthetic anchor could be a small pebble from a favourite forest path.

2   BE YOUR OWN BEST FRIEND/COACH

When things are going wrong, what do you say to yourself? Do you beat yourself up and dwell on those moments when you couldn't deal with a certain child? Do you feel bad that you didn't deal with something perfectly, and wonder if you should really be a teacher?

Now think about what you'd you say to your best friend, if they were in this same situation. You'd no doubt use very different language to the kind of self-talk you use in your mind. You'd probably be supportive, encouraging, and look to the future. Choose to be your own best friend and coach. Be kind to yourself and look after yourself in the same way as you would look after a friend. For example, say to yourself, *"You did your best with that student: take a break and relax now you're home"* rather than thinking, *"That was a really stupid thing to say, you made the situation worse, you need to spend the night planning your lesson better for next time".*

3   FOCUS ON HIGHLIGHTS

At the end of each day, we tend to go home and remember those things which didn't work, the pupils we're not reaching. Whilst some reflection might be necessary, this can be very counter-productive, as we can think ourselves into a pessimistic and negative frame of mind. Dwelling on the failures of the day will make it difficult to face the next day with any enthusiasm.

At the end of each day, take a moment and write down six highlights from your time at school. A highlight doesn't have to be a big thing, it can be a small success. This will **re-frame** your day, and encourage your mind to remain resourceful.

4   FOCUS ON THINGS YOU CAN CONTROL

Take a few minutes and think about all the things you're worried about at the moment, particularly things which may affect your ability to consider new ideas and the processes behind challenging behaviour.

Now make two lists from these - those things you can change and those you can't.

Notice how much of our time is spent on those things over which we have no real control at this precise moment. This is how we can put pressure on ourselves. We spend time focusing on the things we can't change. We need to spend our time on those things that are in our control, in the moment.

5   CREATE THINKING SPACES

In a busy school environment, we need to consciously decide to make time and space for quiet, reflective moments. With pupils who challenge us, we need to take a step back, explore the issue, think differently, try to understand it from different perspectives, and then maybe generate some strategies. Timetable meetings to do this; it will never be time wasted.

6   TALK TO PEOPLE WHO ENERGISE YOU

Arrange to talk to a colleague about your day. Make sure it's a colleague who provides some positive energy, and not someone from whom you will go away feeling negative and hopeless. Allow time for each of you to talk through the events of the day. It's fine to use this time to 'off-load' your feelings and issues, but you need to ensure the final outcome is positive for both of you.

References

Batmanghelidjh, C. *Terrorised and terrorising teenagers - the search for attachment and hope, in,* Perry, A. (2009) *Teenagers and Attachment: Helping adolescents engage with life and learning* London: Worth Publishing

Bion, W. R. (1962a) A theory of thinking *International Journal of Psycho-Analysis*, Vol. 43: Reprinted in Bion, W. R. (1984) *Second Thoughts: Selected Papers on Psychoanalysis* London: Karnac Books

Bombèr, L. M. (2007) *Inside I'm Hurting: Practical strategies for supporting children with attachment difficulties in schools* London: Worth Publishing

Bowlby, J. (1988) *A Secure Base: Clinical applications of Attachment Theory* London: Routledge

Delaney, M. (2009) *Teaching the Unteachable: Practical ideas to give teachers hope and help when behaviour management strategies fail* London: Worth Publishing

Freud, A. (1973) *Normality and Pathology in Childhood* London: Hogarth Press

Gardner, H. (1983, 1993) *Frames of Mind: The theory of multiple intelligences* New York: Basic Books

Geddes, H. (2006) *Attachment in the Classroom: The links between children's early experience, emotional well-being and performance in schools* London: Worth Publishing

Gray, P. & Panter, S. (Feb 2000) Exclusion or inclusion? Perspectives on policy in England for pupils with emotional and behavioural difficulties *Support for Learning,* Vol 15 (1), 4-7

Lawley, J. & Tompkins, P. (2006) *Metaphors in Mind* Lisburn: Developing Company Press

Striker, S. & Kimmel, E. (2007) The *Anti-Colouring Book* Oxford: Scholastic

Sunderland, M. (2001) *A Wibble Called Bipley: A story for children who have hardened their hearts or become bullies* Milton Keynes: Speechmark Publishing

Sunderland, M. (2001) *Willy and the Wobbly House: A story for children who are anxious or obsessional* Milton Keynes: Speechmark Publishing

Sunderland, M. (2003) *How Hattie Hated Kindness: A story for children who are locked in rage and hate* Milton Keynes: Speechmark Publishing

Sunderland, M. (2003) *Teenie Weenie in a Too Big World: A story for fearful children* Milton Keynes: Speechmark Publishing

Terry, R. & Churches, R. (2007) *NLP for Teachers: How to be a highly effective teacher* New York: Crown House Publishing

Winnicott, D. W. (1971) *Playing and Reality* London: Routledge

Index